12-06			

JOE SACCO

MONICA MARSHALL

The Rosen Publishing Group, Inc., New York

To all people who want to live in peace

Published in 2005 by The Rosen Publishing Group, Inc.
29 East 21st Street, New York, NY 10010

First Edition

Library of Congress Cataloging-in-Publication Data

Marshall, Monica.
Joe Sacco / by Monica Marshall.
    p. cm. — (The library of graphic novelists)
Includes bibliographical references and index.
ISBN 1-4042-0284-6 (library binding)
1. Sacco, Joe. 2. Cartoonists—United States—Biography.
I. Title. II. Series.
PN6727.S14M37 2004
741.5'092—dc22

2004016654

Manufactured in Malaysia

CONTENTS

With profound compassion, cartoonist and journalist Joe Sacco speaks for those who have no voice. He appears in his comic books as a bespectacled and unassuming character who gently informs his readers but is never self-righteous. With his hands sometimes in his pockets, he wanders from frame to frame, retelling the painful stories of Palestinian and Bosnian refugees, or reconstructing the history of modern warfare. If there is humor among the misery, he eagerly embraces it.

Driven by a will to let the stories of the people organically unfold, Sacco travels, notebook in hand, from interview to interview, sipping tea and listening intently to whatever information is shared. One can easily see how a battered and shaken people would have an immediate trust in him: Sacco is a selfless observer, someone who carefully listens first and evaluates later. These character traits helped earn him the

Joe Sacco commonly draws himself as a character in his comics stories, like he is seen here, in a drawing that was originally featured inside the cover of the fifth issue of *Palestine*, first printed in 1994. Armed with nothing more than a desire to let the Palestinians speak for themselves, Sacco joined them in their homes and refugee camps and listened to their stories for several months during the winter of 1991 and 1992. He eventually produced nine serialized comics about the Palestinian struggle that were later compiled into the book *Palestine* in 1996.

street credibility to get the story firsthand, directly from the people who have experienced it.

Although he originally had the desire for a job as a foreign news correspondent, Sacco forged his own path as a journalist by sharing his unique style of comics drawing. His first foray into his self-styled role of comics journalist was in the comic-book series *Palestine*, which first appeared in 1993. He is both empathetic and passionate as he tells the story of the Palestinian people during the end of the first uprising. Block by block, Sacco takes readers into his world to share an intimacy with difficult subject matter. The effect is a stunning achievement that broke the traditional comics superhero mold. The late Columbia professor of Middle Eastern studies Edward Said called *Palestine* "a political and aesthetic work of extraordinary originality" when he wrote the introduction to the collected edition, which later appeared as a book in 1996.

Eventually, Sacco wrote and illustrated other pioneering works of nonfiction comics, including *Safe Area Gorazde: The War in Eastern Bosnia 1992–95* (2000), and *The Fixer: A Story from Sarajevo* (2003). Another book, *Notes from a Defeatist*, which is a collection of earlier autobiographical works, also appeared in 2003 to critical acclaim. After many years of restless traveling, Sacco has finally settled down in Portland, Oregon, where he can be found in the back of a roomy old house, listening to jazz and the blues, and drawing his latest comics.

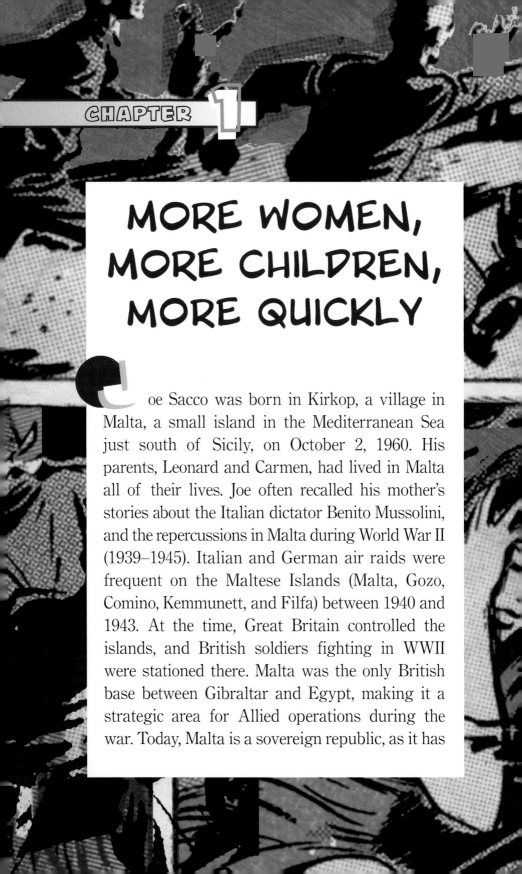

CHAPTER 1

MORE WOMEN, MORE CHILDREN, MORE QUICKLY

oe Sacco was born in Kirkop, a village in Malta, a small island in the Mediterranean Sea just south of Sicily, on October 2, 1960. His parents, Leonard and Carmen, had lived in Malta all of their lives. Joe often recalled his mother's stories about the Italian dictator Benito Mussolini, and the repercussions in Malta during World War II (1939–1945). Italian and German air raids were frequent on the Maltese Islands (Malta, Gozo, Comino, Kemmunett, and Filfa) between 1940 and 1943. At the time, Great Britain controlled the islands, and British soldiers fighting in WWII were stationed there. Malta was the only British base between Gibraltar and Egypt, making it a strategic area for Allied operations during the war. Today, Malta is a sovereign republic, as it has been since 1964, when it gained its independence from Great Britain.

At the start of World War II, however, Carmen Sacco was only six years old. Her tales of the death and destruction from bombs that fell during air raids later influenced her family, especially her son Joe. Carmen Sacco recounted stories about how Maltese families had banded together in shelters and lived from rationed foods, and how she was one of the few children who managed to get to school, which was in Valletta, the capital of Malta.

In January 1941, the Luftwaffe, the German air force, part of the Axis powers, often flew over Malta. That same year, the Luftwaffe started using bombs against the British soldiers who were stationed on the islands. Thousands of bombs fell in Malta during the conflict, and more than 1,500 Maltese civilians were killed. While Joe Sacco must have been horrified as a child when listening to his mother's stories about the war, something inside his mind was intensely fueled by the pride and perseverance of the Maltese people. Later, Sacco realized how much of his mother's past helped shape his decisions to listen to others' war stories. Later, as an adult, he became intensely curious about how people survived in occupied territories. He was continuously interested in learning about how the displacement of people due to these conflicts affected the relationships between nations. He would later retell his mother's stories in a comic format. Based on letters that she wrote about her experiences, Sacco drew "More Women, More Children, More Quickly" in 1990. The title was taken from a quote by the former British prime minister

In this first panel of *A Disgusting Experience*, Sacco looks back and examines his life, beginning by recounting details of his family's move from Malta to Australia when he was a small child. First drawn in 1989, it marks one of Sacco's first stories with a political theme. *A Disgusting Experience* was later reprinted in *Notes From a Defeatist*, an anthology of early work that came out in 2003.

Stanley Baldwin. Baldwin said, as Sacco recounted in his comic, "I think it is well for the man in the street to realize that there is no power on earth that can protect him from being bombed . . . The bomber will always get through. The only defense is offense, which means that you have to kill more women and children more quickly than the enemy if you want to save yourselves."

The Sacco family, including Maryanne Sacco, Joe's older sister, immigrated to Australia in 1961, shortly after Joe was born. Australia has a policy of allowing large-scale immigration, like the United States and Canada do, so many Maltese settled there throughout the 1950s and 1960s. Australia was an attractive choice for the Saccos because of its warm climate. Together the family lived in a small suburb of Melbourne, near the coast, and Sacco's mother, Carmen, took a job as a high school teacher. Sacco's memories of Australia are dim, but he does recall having friends of mixed nationality. Nearly all of them were European-born, or had European-born parents. All of his friends' parents remembered WWII, and often discussed the impact the conflict had had on their families. It seemed that even in Australia, Sacco could not escape learning about a war that had changed so many lives. He listened carefully to the harrowing stories of near misses and suffering, and to some extent, over-glorified the idea of war and nationalism. Even the comics that he read at this time were British war comics that his father would buy him in downtown Melbourne. The military prowess of any country fascinated Sacco as a child, but the military strength of the United States seemed the most glorious of all.

Sacco drew inspiration from his mother's personal memories for the 1990 comics story "More Women, More Children, More Quickly," which retold her horrifying experiences in Malta during World War II. To accurately portray Carmen Sacco's experiences, Sacco had his mother recount her memory of the war in a series of letters that he then used to help him construct the comic's basic framework. "More Women" was later reprinted in *Notes from a Defeatist* in 2003.

By his sixth birthday, Sacco had begun drawing crude characters that were fashioned after popular comic-book heroes of the day. In an interview with the public television arts program *EGG*, he recalled telling stories as a child with pictures and no words. Once, when his mother was in the hospital, Joe and his sister, Maryanne, wanted to make a present for her, so together they fashioned a homemade comic book. Although it was based loosely on a popular British comic character of the period, it represented one of Sacco's first pieces of sequential art.

War Stories

While Sacco played war with his friends in Australia, American men and women were fighting an actual war in Southeast Asia. The conflict in Vietnam began in the late 1950s, between Communist North Vietnam and non-Communist South Vietnam, both of which were once the French colony of Indochina. The United States' involvement in Vietnam came later, during the 1960s and the 1970s, around the time that Sacco first came to the United States from Australia. According to then-president John F. Kennedy, who was later assassinated in 1963, before the end of his term, the United States entered the war to control the spread of Communism, a directive that had been in place since the late 1950s. As the years passed and fighting by the Vietcong worsened, President Kennedy's successor, Lyndon B. Johnson, sent more American men and women to fight what appeared to be an unending war.

A war photographer in Saigon, in South Vietnam, took this photograph of a homeless mother and child in 1967 during the Vietnam War (1961–1975). Hundreds of thousands of Vietnamese were displaced during the conflict, as entire villages were extinguished during the crossfire between the Vietcong and U.S. troops. Some historians estimate that millions of Vietnamese lost their lives during the war.

American involvement in Vietnam became increasingly controversial as more lives were lost. Soon, massive demonstrations against the war were seen regularly under President Richard Nixon, who took office in 1968. Nixon decreased American troops in the region. He tried to negotiate a cease-fire agreement after it seemed that the combined forces of the United States and South Vietnam were useless against the Communist North Vietnamese. But the insurgency of the Communist troops and the plight of the South Vietnamese didn't strike a chord in Sacco the way that other conflicts had before or since.

In a 1995 interview in the *Comics Journal*, Sacco said, "I wasn't paying too much attention to Vietnam [until] there was a friend of my family who was in the reserves and [we] were worried about him going over to Vietnam." News of war stories brought the conflict into greater focus. Sacco also recalled some of the striking and horrific television footage and still photographs of the war. Like most Americans, he was revolted by a series of images, taken by Nick Ut in 1972, of Asian children suffering from the effects of napalm that was dropped on their village by the South Vietnamese air force. For Sacco, and anyone else who witnessed the war in this way, it became an all-too-real nightmare.

Still, Sacco's position as a young man was strikingly conservative. He didn't participate in protests against the war or speak out against the conflict. He remembered coming to the United States prior to the presidential election of 1972, and hearing young people argue about who should become president—Nixon, the incumbent, or Democrat George McGovern, who was a pacifist. He remembered being in favor of Nixon simply because he had already held the highest office. But U.S. politics held little interest for Sacco at the time, and he instead remained focused on his hobbies, which at this time included following other conflicts around the world, comics, and military history.

By this point, Sacco had been drawing his own comics and illustrating stories that he had written. "When I started drawing as a child, I almost immediately started drawing comics," Sacco recounted in a 2001 interview on www.sequentialtart.com. "For some reason, I wanted to tell stories, and I used pictures to tell them. I did my first comic book when I was six or seven years old." As Sacco grew, so did his artistic ambitions, though it wasn't until he hit his twenties that he considered giving up a "regular" job to try to make it as a comic-book artist.

Meanwhile, during Carmen Sacco's stint as a high school teacher in Australia, Sacco remembered meeting one of her colleagues, an Egyptian teacher who spoke to him about conflicts in the Middle East. Soon their conversations turned to the 1967 Six-Day War that saw Israeli forces attack Egypt and Syria. Troops from Jordan also entered the conflict, and Israeli forces quickly and efficiently defeated all Arab troops. The Israel Defense Forces made its presence known as the most dominant military force in the region. In doing so, Israel took control of the West Bank (formally controlled by Jordan), the Gaza Strip and the Sinai Peninsula (formally controlled by Egypt), and the Golan Heights (formally controlled by Syria). At the time, Sacco was only seven years old. He also recalled discussions with his friends regarding the war between India and Pakistan in 1971 that led to the liberation of Bangladesh. Although he was not fully aware of the history between the two nations, he had a higher awareness of how people were fighting for their rights around the world. At the same time, Sacco dreamed of living an idyllic, carefree lifestyle in the United States. He imagined clean and manicured suburban neighborhoods, riding his very own bicycle, and playing with friends. Having grown up watching several American television programs overseas, Sacco thought that living in the United States resembled what he had seen on television.

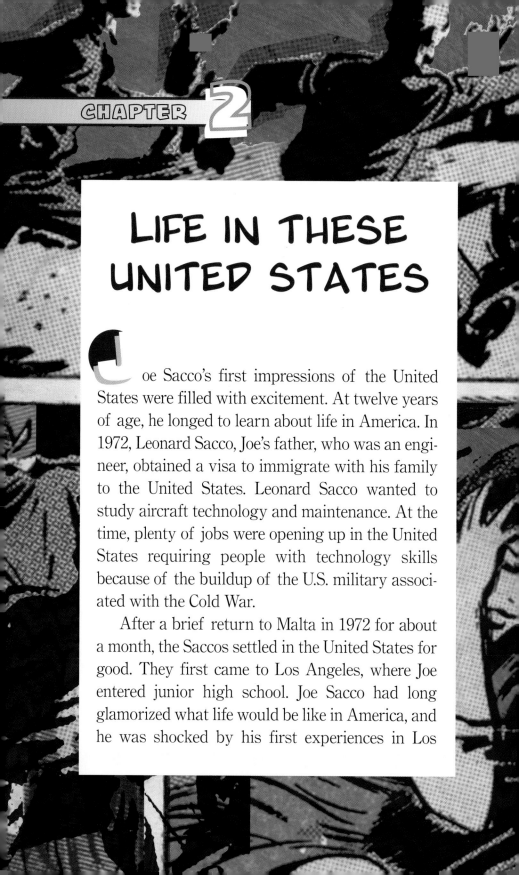

CHAPTER 2

LIFE IN THESE UNITED STATES

Joe Sacco's first impressions of the United States were filled with excitement. At twelve years of age, he longed to learn about life in America. In 1972, Leonard Sacco, Joe's father, who was an engineer, obtained a visa to immigrate with his family to the United States. Leonard Sacco wanted to study aircraft technology and maintenance. At the time, plenty of jobs were opening up in the United States requiring people with technology skills because of the buildup of the U.S. military associated with the Cold War.

After a brief return to Malta in 1972 for about a month, the Saccos settled in the United States for good. They first came to Los Angeles, where Joe entered junior high school. Joe Sacco had long glamorized what life would be like in America, and he was shocked by his first experiences in Los

Angeles. Living in a small apartment on La Tijera Boulevard in Inglewood, about ten miles (sixteen kilometers) from downtown LA, he experienced racial tensions between African Americans and whites that were before unknown to him. He remembers being disturbed by the frequent and disruptive fighting that occurred on the school bus, for instance. Sacco recalls junior high school students who often picked fights and others who frequently took drugs. He even befriended a student whose brother was murdered; the brother had been the victim of gun violence.

Racial tensions had been on the rise for years in LA, a city that had been racially divided since the 1940s. Mexicans and African Americans were drawn to the area in large numbers and frequently suffered from discrimination, as did most minority groups in cities across the United States, including recent immigrants from Europe. During the 1960s, the African American population in LA swelled to 500,000, and blacks predominated in South Central LA and Watts County. Only seven years earlier, in 1965, Watts had been the site of massive race riots that had been sparked by an alleged beating of an African American by two white California police officers. Thirty-four deaths had occurred as a result of the spree of violence that escalated over six days and destroyed approximately 11 square miles (28 sq. km) of property. The fighting and damages totaled more than $40 million.

On one particular occasion in 1973, Sacco even found himself in the middle of a fight between LA

In this photograph taken in Los Angeles shortly after the Watts riots in August 1965, a member of the National Guard patrols the barren streets where businesses, razed to the ground during the violent outbreak, once stood. Although Sacco and his family moved to the Los Angeles area several years after the conflict, racial tensions there were still commonplace.

gang members. He had stepped off a school bus into a crowd of black students, when a smaller bunch of whites exited a nearby car and pulled guns on the crowd. Fortunately, Sacco and his friends escaped without incident. It would not be the last time that he would be found in harm's way.

In other respects, America seemed like a place where people were extremely nationalistic, another striking memory for Sacco. One of his first impressions of the United States occurred during the drive from Los Angeles International Airport to the home of family friends. Although the Saccos' stay in Los Angeles was only temporary, the impression made on Sacco was that the United States was a place where people were extremely patriotic. While he might not have immediately connected the elevated sense of patriotism with America's support of its troops in Vietnam, the connection later became apparent. During the short trip to the LA suburb, Sacco remembered seeing more American flags than he could have counted.

Portland

In 1974, the Saccos moved north from California to Oregon. They settled in Beaverton, a suburb of Portland, which is a city that would later figure largely in Sacco's life and career. Oregon was a change of pace for Sacco. Beaverton was a small town full of open spaces and families who were financially well situated. Sacco, now fourteen, entered Sunset High School, where he was first introduced to journalism. The school was progressive; its mission statement read, "[Sunset High School] is a challenging educational community [that promotes] lifelong learning, social responsibility, and respect for diversity." Unlike the school kids in LA, the kids in Beaverton were less aggressive and more open-minded to people from other cultures. There were far fewer disagreements over race and less competition for home turf. Before long, Sacco got involved with the school paper, the *Sunset Scroll*. At first, he found himself drawing editorial cartoons, but within weeks, Sacco had a regular byline as a contributing writer. His favorite pieces were short biographies based on interviews he had done with students who grew up in foreign nations. Sacco's intense interest in writing and documenting the students' lifestyles was an early glimpse into how he would shape his future. Just before graduating from Sunset in 1978, Sacco shaped the writing in the entire *Scroll* by acting as its managing editor for a semester. This was around the same time that he began to take seriously the idea of becoming a professional journalist. Although he was still drawing cartoons for fun, he did not consider his artistic abilities very marketable. One of his early attempts at a comic book was a story he called *A Fistful of Tequila*, which profiled the lives of several Mexican bandits. Looking back, he thinks it was one of the pieces that really helped shape his current style. Intrigued by the extreme close-ups that were part of the violent Clint Eastwood film *A Fistful of Dollars*, Sacco chose to make his characters as ugly as possible.

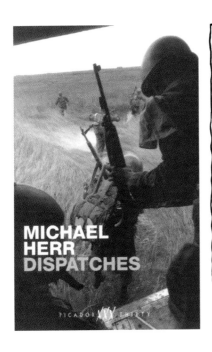

MICHAEL
HERR
DISPATCHES

"I was cartooning all the time, since I was a kid, but I remember when I got in high school I got in journalism class and I really enjoyed it. I enjoyed writing articles and interviewing people and getting quotes," Sacco recounts in the *Comics Journal.*

Sacco graduated Sunset High School in 1978, with a career in journalism on his mind. In the fall of that same year, he entered the University of Oregon in Eugene, where he enrolled in its School of Journalism and Communication. The university at first inspired Sacco, and he filled his days with classes in feature writing, reporting, and editing, and drawing the occasional comic for the *Oregon Daily Emerald*, the university newspaper. Sacco had set his sights on eventually becoming a foreign news correspondent. At the time, one of his heroes was the American journalist Michael Herr, who was stationed in Vietnam from 1967 to 1969. Herr's book, *Dispatches*, is often praised as being one of the best pieces of writing on modern warfare. Herr's prose was eloquent, even when his subject matter was not, and he never shied away from exposing the war for exactly what it was: a deadly, bloody battle. Herr combined his poetic prose with song lyrics of the period like those of Bob Dylan, the Rolling Stones, and Jimi Hendrix (similar to Sacco's rock influences), which also made it into narrative and helped give the book a striking sociological perspective. Sacco was incredibly moved by Herr's writing, as well as by the writing of George Orwell and Hunter S. Thompson—all authors have been important influences. In some cases, Sacco's exposure to these authors helped fuel his existing interest to recount the tragic stories about tortured or displaced people. By this time, Sacco had developed a high level of respect for writers who learned directly from firsthand experience.

Although the University of Oregon was and is widely respected as one of the oldest educational institutions that teaches journalism, Sacco soon felt his college experience lacked substance. It seemed that he held a greater integrity toward the pursuit of journalism than many of his professors had. These unfulfilled expectations made him think of college more as a standardized experience and less as an individual one focused on personal growth. Because Sacco wanted to get out into the world of professional journalism, he rushed to finish the program early and graduated from the university in 1981. He had earned his bachelor's degree in three years instead of four.

During spring and summer breaks and weekends when he wasn't studying, Sacco spent his time drawing comics, though he still didn't consider the possibility of making a living from his art. Eventually, he set out to finish documenting the history of the Vietnam War, a project that he started during the late 1970s. Sacco filled hour upon hour writing about what he thought had gone wrong with the war and American politics in general. It became an epic comic that he would completely reshape several times as he matured, his viewpoints evolved, and his skills as an artist sharpened. Years earlier, in his teens, he had been quite inspired by comics that re-created historical events, such as those that depicted highlights of the American Revolution. His favorites were those that not only retold history in comic form, but made fun of it as well.

"Actually, the first comic I remember looking at and thinking, 'Oh, this is different,' was called *Bicentennial Gross Outs* [which] was a comic [by William Stout] about American intervention in the Philippines that was really wild and political and amazing," Sacco recalled in *The Comics Journal*. Since he had never been interested in superheroes, Sacco's comic radar was on the make for something unique, or a groundbreaking treatment of the ordinary. Stout's powerful treatment of U.S. actions during the Philippine-American War (1899–1902), and his realistic and detailed drawings immediately resonated with Sacco, who had before not paid too much attention to the underground comics scene.

A History of Underground Comics

The underground comics (sometimes referred to as comix) movement of the 1960s and 1970s describes the period when the first widespread independent, self-published comic titles were produced. Unlike the commercial comics offerings that were widely available at supermarket newsstands, these limited-run comics were mostly found in underground shops.

The underground comics movement was centered on the West Coast, specifically in San Francisco. Its artists were frustrated at earlier restrictions placed on their work by the Comics Code Authority (CCA). This was a self-regulating agency created by comics artists of the 1950s. They developed a specific code for any questionable content that might be found in comics publishers, a response to an outrageous book by Dr. Fredric Wertham called *Seduction of the Innocent* (1954). Wertham's book caused such a stir with the American public that the U.S. Senate held hearings to investigate its claims. The CCA was created by publishers out of fear that the entire industry would be brought down by Wertham's accusations. He believed that some of the comics of the 1950s, such as the titles *Shock SuspenStories* and *Tomb of Terror* were corrupting America's youth with ruthlessly violence themes. Entertaining Comics (EC) suffered the worst damage and was forced to kill a large percentage of its titles including *Vault of Horror* and *Tales from the Crypt.*

Rather than be censored by the CCA code, many comics artists of the 1960s underground scene decided to self-publish their wares. These artists were heavily influenced by the earlier EC comics and Harvey Kurtzman's *Mad* magazine. Most of their titles' content revolved around the hippie, counterculture, and psychedelic scene. Common themes included those of a sexual nature, buying and using illegal drugs, and avoiding pressure or capture by the local police. Some of the more prominent comics artists associated with this movement included Robert Crumb (*Zap Comix, Hytone, Despair*), Gilbert Shelton (*The Fabulous Furry Freak Brothers*), Robert Williams (*Coochie Cootie's Men's Comics*), Bill Griffith and Art Spiegelman (*Arcade*), Rick Griffin (*Tales from the Tube*), and Kim Deitch (*Corn Fed*).

The accusations of explicit content, however, did not end with Wertham's 1954 book. In the early 1970s, Robert Crumb was prosecuted for material produced in *Zap* number 4 that was considered obscene. After numerous appeals, the issue was ruled obscene in 1974 and banned. But that didn't stop underground artists from creating comix with an adult edge. Other artists developed out of the movement, too, and some moved into the alternative comics scene of the 1980s once the underground era ebbed.

Even as the mainstream comics put out by DC and Marvel survived and flourished over the years, the underground scene did not. In the 1980s, underground comix became known as alternative comics. They were still published independently of the major publishing houses, and still in limited press runs, but they enjoyed a lively following and grew in popularity. Often produced by one or two individuals, alternative comics titles catered to specialized groups.

One of the more striking titles to emerge during this period was *RAW*, an anthology of alternative comics artists that was produced in a large format by Art Spiegelman and his wife, Françoise Mouly. Spiegelman and Mouly helped pave the way for unknown artists, including Mark Beyer, Chris Ware, Daniel Clowes, Charles Burns, David Mazzuchelli, J. Otto Seibold, and Kaz. Other popular titles of the 1980s were *Love & Rockets*, the Hernandez brothers' comic that profiled the Latino scene in Los Angeles, and Harvey Pekar's comic of everyday life, *American Splendor*. Another important development in the alternative scene was the establishment of the publishing house Fantagraphics, which would eventually put out material by Joe Sacco.

Gary Groth and Kim Thompson started Fantagraphics in a Los Angeles suburb in the late 1970s. By the 1990s, however, the company moved to Seattle and was almost solely responsible for embracing the growing audience for alternative comics. They also established the first professional journal of the industry, the *Comics Journal*, where Sacco worked as a writer/reporter in the mid-1980s. Today, Fantagraphics publishes a variety of cutting-edge comic artists including the Hernandez brothers, Daniel Clowes, Roberta Gregory, and Stan Sakai. It also publishes comic reprints of important work, including a complete library of Robert Crumb's sketchbooks and retrospective books featuring the works of the syndicated artists George Herriman (*Krazy Kat*), and Charles Schulz (*Peanuts*).

Meanwhile, as the alternative West Coast comics scene was slowly gaining momentum, Sacco continued searching for a meaningful job in publishing. It was 1981, and he was seeking a position as a staff writer or editor, but opportunities did not come easily. Looking back, he realized that the journalism market had reached a saturation point as many young people fresh out of college were also looking for their own bylines. In Sacco's opinion, the earlier excitement of going undercover and exposing a national story like President Nixon's involvement in the Watergate scandal of the 1970s had made journalism seem even more exciting. Young people really wanted the chance to reach the public with hard-hitting and meaningful news stories.

"I think the whole glamour of the Watergate journalists really made people interested in that career, so there was a glut of people [in the journalism market]," he said in an 1995 interview in the *Comics Journal*. But finding a job where he could pursue his immediate goals of reporting on world politics and events was impossible, and instead Sacco found that he was repeatedly offered writing positions at small newsletters and trade magazines. Soon he found himself moving back in with his parents, who were then living in Thousand Oaks, an upper-middle-class suburb of Los Angeles. For a while, at least, it seemed that Sacco was not going to find the dream job for which he had been looking. Instead of taking any position as a writer, he made due for a few months with light factory jobs.

This was the early 1980s, around the time that the first copies of Spiegelman's critically acclaimed *RAW*

hit the presses. *RAW*, like the earlier *Arcade* (assembled and edited by Spiegelman and Griffith) was a forum for up-and-coming comic talents to strut their stuff. Spiegelman's best-known comic work is a Pulitzer Prize-winning graphic novel about the Holocaust called *Maus*, which was first published as a serialized comic in *RAW*.

Since *RAW*, Spiegelman's name is now synonymous with mainstream comic success.

After seeing such a bold entry into the comic world, Sacco submitted some of his own comics to *RAW*, only to be turned down. He recalls reading a form letter that tried to be encouraging, but was, at the same time, actually a letter of rejection. Instead of giving up his dreams of publishing comics, the rejection inspired Sacco, who then became even more motivated. While *RAW* commonly featured East Coast artists, Sacco was just slowly becoming aware of the growing West Coast comics scene, of which he would soon be a part.

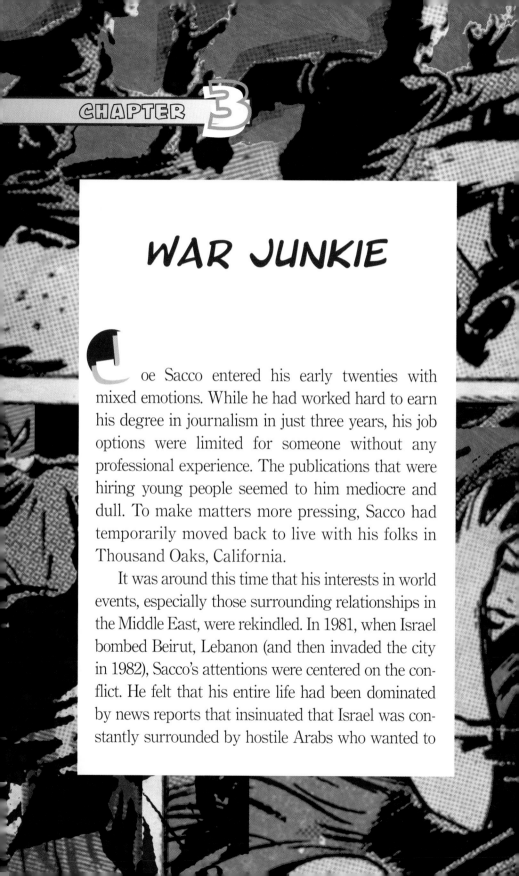

CHAPTER 3

WAR JUNKIE

oe Sacco entered his early twenties with mixed emotions. While he had worked hard to earn his degree in journalism in just three years, his job options were limited for someone without any professional experience. The publications that were hiring young people seemed to him mediocre and dull. To make matters more pressing, Sacco had temporarily moved back to live with his folks in Thousand Oaks, California.

It was around this time that his interests in world events, especially those surrounding relationships in the Middle East, were rekindled. In 1981, when Israel bombed Beirut, Lebanon (and then invaded the city in 1982), Sacco's attentions were centered on the conflict. He felt that his entire life had been dominated by news reports that insinuated that Israel was constantly surrounded by hostile Arabs who wanted to

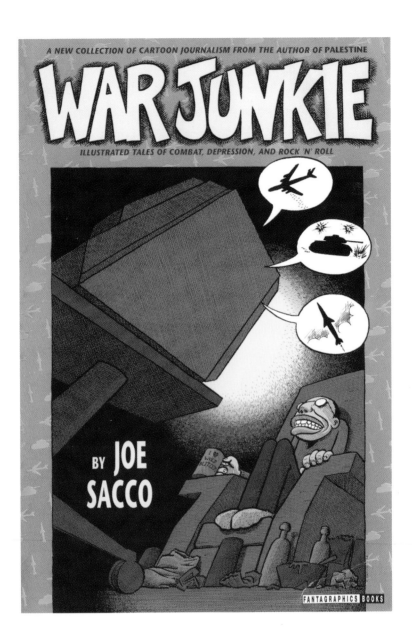

Joe Sacco is depicted on the cover of his 1995 comic book *War Junkie*, while holding a coffee mug that says "I love Wolf Blitzer." Blitzer is a correspondent for CNN who covered the Gulf War in 1991. Meant as a playful joke, Sacco is letting his readers know how much he was absorbed by the United States' media coverage of the war. *War Junkie* featured many of the comics stories that were later reprinted in *Notes From a Defeatist* in 2003.

destroy the country and gain back their land that was lost in the 1967 war. Sacco began to question Israel's authority because he felt that the bombing in Lebanon was unjust. After all, the Israelis were using weaponry that was provided by the United States for "defensive" purposes. These feelings of injustice, combined with the 1982 massacre of between 2,000 and 3,000 Lebanese and Palestinians by the Israeli-allied Christian Lebanese militia at the Palestinian refugee camps of Sabra and Shatila, influenced Sacco, and he wanted to learn more. He wondered about America's relationship with Israel and began to question the coverage of these and other events on the television news and in newspapers such as the *Los Angeles* and the *New York Times*. Sacco validated some of these opinions after reading books like Noam Chomsky's *The Fateful Triangle*, which examined the history of the relationship between Israelis and Palestinians and how they have been portrayed in major American newspapers, specifically in the *New York Times*. To help him understand more about the situation in Palestine, Sacco started immersing himself in books about the Middle East, including Said's *The Question of Palestine, Orientalism*, and *Blaming the Victims*. It wasn't as if Sacco had formed a biased opinion that all Palestinians were justified in their actions. He firmly believes, for instance, that acts of terrorism by both Palestinians and Israelis are unjustified and horrific, but having grown up in America, Sacco became skeptical that he wasn't always learning of these world events in a way that was fully objective.

Meanwhile, he continued his job search. After about six months of hunting, Sacco took a job with the journal

While exploring the art of the shorter narrative, Joe Sacco created a number of unlikely characters, such as Stanton K. Pragmatron, who was featured in a series of strips that created parodies out of working in various environments like small offices and libraries. Most of these shorter, semiautobiographical pieces originally appeared in *Yahoo*.

of the National Notary Association, an unlikely writing position for someone so keen on writing hard news. The journal was written and assembled specifically for public notaries, people who make a living as witnesses and who sign important documents such as bills of sale, living wills, and so forth. The magazine's sole purpose was to inform its readers about changes within the industry and to sell items that notaries might need, such as personalized seals, self-inking stamps, and the like.

Although Sacco and the other employees at the company were extremely professional about the work, it was hard to ignore that the magazine was only important to public notaries. It was far from what Sacco wanted for his future in journalism. Still, the position lasted thirteen months and earned him his first professional writing credentials. It was a starting point from which to search for something better. Soon he found that the banter of his coworkers, the ins and outs of working in an office environment, and the act of putting together a magazine fascinated him, despite the fact that the writing was, as he described it, "exceedingly boring." Later, he claimed that constant office humor surrounding the experience made its way into his early comic work like *Tales of the Office* and *White Collar Incursion*, both of which were later included in the comic series *Yahoo* and in an anthology of Sacco's early work. *Notes from a Defeatist* was released in 2003, and along with stand-alone comic tales that were derived from his first professional jobs, it also included the works that would eventually evolve into longer pieces of comic journalism like "When Good Bombs Happen to Bad People."

Return to Malta

Within a year of starting his first job, Sacco felt a need to return to his homeland. Malta became an independent republic shortly after his family had left for Australia, and Sacco wanted to return to his roots. He remembered a short visit to the island when he was twelve years old, and another while he was on break from the University of Oregon. Now he wanted to see if he could make a permanent life in Malta. When he left, he remembered feeling obsessed with the idea of making a new life for himself in Europe.

Like it was then, Malta is a European island that thrives mostly on tourism. The Maltese live mostly in small villages and in larger cities of no more than about 15,000 people. They speak English and Maltese, both of which are official languages. Malta is self-sufficient and industrialized after having been under the control of the British from the early nineteenth century. Besides a growing tourism industry, the Maltese Islands are known for their textile businesses and thriving harbors.

Sacco loved being back in his homeland and quickly got a writing job for a local publisher. He wrote a travel guidebook about Malta. Finally, he felt some sense of purpose with his professional writing work and was pleased to be making a living in publishing. Soon his contacts led to other opportunities such as feature-writing assignments for a magazine called *Tomorrow*.

Although it was essentially a business publication, it was Sacco's first chance to write about news that he felt was important. His stories were hard-hitting, built from investigative interviews. Sacco was finally in his element. He interviewed young Maltese men who had repeated relations with female foreigners in Malta who came to the island specifically for that purpose. He also interviewed unemployed men and women known for earning cash tips rather than reporting and paying taxes on declared wages, a crime known in Malta as working "in the black." For Sacco, the experience was priceless. It was the first time since high school that he had shaped his writing from interviews, and he loved the process as much in Malta as he had in Oregon. The Maltese trusted Sacco because he was one of their own. His friendly nature led them to reveal details about themselves that gave his writing a particular edge. Soon, however, Sacco's interests in writing commercially would merge with his private talent for drawing comics. Before long, the publisher that once had Sacco writing about Maltese beaches would have him devoting his time to something far more lucrative: creating romance comics.

At first, the idea of using comics to tell a romantic story seemed hilarious to Sacco, who had only used his drawings to recount historical events such as the Vietnam War. Since the publisher offered him a good deal, he embraced the project. He ran with the idea of writing and illustrating romance comics and knocked them out at a steady pace. In all, Sacco wrote and illustrated six full issues; three while he was in Malta, and three after he'd returned to the United States. Each was sixty-four pages long and half the trim size of a traditional American comic book. Sacco had to write the story, translate it into Maltese with the help of a relative, and do the drawings, all within the span of one month. He remembers working at a frenzied pace, drawing something like five to seven pages each day. Looking back, he credits the rigorous schedule with helping him get the feel for working on a deadline, something he now enjoys.

In order to keep his residency from expiring in the United States, Sacco moved back to America after nearly a year, and continued drawing romance comics from Portland. Unfortunately, although the comics sold well, Sacco was only partially paid for his work. Now broke and living on his own, Sacco took a temporary job as a proofreader at a local law firm.

For Sacco, Portland was a good fit. It had both a thriving downtown and the privacy of the open landscape. A city of nature lovers, Portland is known for its friendly, politically minded folk, their grass-roots activism, and rainy weather. Portland, like most of the Northwest, sees an average of 150 days per year of rainfall, something that most artists of the thriving West Coast comics scene say helps them meet the time-dwindling demand of all those drawings. (Years later, Sacco often commented that for him, Portland was a city of few distractions, unlike New York, where he later moved in 2001.)

Once settled, Sacco jumped to another editorial position, this one as a copy editor for a local magazine in downtown Portland. *The Downtowner* catered to advertisers and local businesses, and it was far from the editorial position Sacco had envisioned for himself. Struggling to find meaning in his work, and concerned about his future as a writer, Sacco was becoming discouraged. The only idea that lifted his spirits was the thought that he might one day publish his own magazine.

Portland Permanent Press

By 1985, Sacco had been out of college for several years. His publishing jobs were many, though none had left him feeling very fulfilled. Along the way, he had learned valuable skills in layout, typography, design, copyediting, preparing documents for printing, and maintaining rigorous deadlines. Just as important, he had also saved money and made a few friends in the industry. One of his friends was Tom Richards, who also had a lot of publishing experience and wanted to start his own publication. Because they both were interested in self-publishing, they decided to combine their skills on a monthly humor magazine they named *Portland Permanent Press* (PPP).

PPP was meant to cover the growing downtown comedy scene in Portland and introduce up-and-coming stand-up talent as well as budding print cartoonists, including Sacco himself. The print work was varied. It featured interviews with some artists whose later work would become very well-known, such as Matt Groening of *The Simpsons* fame, who, at the time, serialized a strip called *Life in Hell*. It also included early comic panels from John Callahan, a quadriplegic who creates irreverent humor about the handicapped; J. R. Williams, creator of *Bummer*; and Peter Bagge, who was then editing Robert Crumb's *Weirdo* before creating *Neat Stuff* and *Hate*. Sacco, who before had not known much about the world of alternative comics, was slowly getting introduced to some of its main West Coast players.

But the thrill of compiling and editing a monthly magazine was short-lived. The publication was free, so it depended heavily on revenue from ad sales, something Richards had a lot of experience with in the past, though he spent the majority of his efforts trying to help Sacco keep *PPP* afloat. At the time, it was one of the only free monthly publications in Portland. Soon, Sacco's energy and savings were tapped, and both he and Richards took part-time jobs to help meet printing costs. Sacco went to work as a mail sorter, and Richards found a position in a copy shop. After a few more months, and little improvement in cash flow, *PPP* folded in 1986. The final decision came after Sacco's car broke down and he could no longer distribute the paper. He was completely out of cash.

But with conflict came opportunity. When Sacco began calling businesses who had placed ads to say that *PPP* was no longer accepting new ads, one of those advertisers, Fantagraphics, offered him a job at their publication, the *Comics Journal*, a monthly magazine about the artists and goings-on in the comics industry. Because Sacco now had a working knowledge of the Northwest comics scene, it seemed like a good fit. He then moved back to California where he would spend the next seven months.

Kim Thompson and Gary Groth, founders of the comics publishing house known as Fantagraphics, in their Seattle office. Both Groth and Thompson employed Sacco during his twenties and were the publishers of his early comic work. Sacco met Groth and Thompson while working as a writer/reporter for the *Comics Journal*, a quarterly publication of the comics and cartoonists industry put out by Fantagraphics.

Fantagraphics

At the time, Fantagraphics was a tiny company located in a suburb of Los Angeles that had been around since 1976. (Fantagraphics moved to Seattle, Washington, in 1989.) Sacco wore many hats at the

Journal, but his favorite was that of a writer, covering newsworthy items for its front section on important issues facing comics artists, such as censorship. Meanwhile, he continued writing and drawing a new version of his Vietnam comic epic, which was then about fifty pages long. At one point, it occurred to Sacco to show his drawings to Fantagraphics owners Gary Groth and Kim Thompson. At the time, they were publishing a handful of alternative comic artists like Peter Bagge (*Neat Stuff, Hate*) and the Hernandez brothers, Jaime, Gilbert, and Mario (*Love and Rockets*). But Sacco's work was very different from the popular comics of the day. There were few memorable characters, and the work lacked an obvious beginning, middle, and end. It was very rough. Groth's response to Sacco's efforts was discouraging, but it helped Sacco put his work into perspective. Sacco had drawn and redrawn the comic for six or seven years by that point, and he needed to take a step back. He decided to switch gears to draw socially relevant comics that were shorter and more topical. Soon Sacco submitted work to other comic publishers such as Kitchen Sink and Rip Off Press. Even though all his work was rejected, Sacco was somehow inspired to pursue his art. It was around this time that he decided he wanted to earn a living from writing and drawing comics.

"I realized that cartooning was in my blood. I'd been doing it all the time, and not for reasons of making money," he said in the *Comics Journal.* "I just enjoyed doing it. I enjoyed drawing. The thing is, if I had made it as a journalist, as a writer, I would have gone with that and [only] done cartooning as a hobby or just for fun or for a friend. I love writing, too. It's a different kind of thing, though."

During his first year at Fantagraphics, more opportunities to get involved with comics arose for Sacco. Soon he began editing issues of a magazine called *Honk!*, originally by Tom Mason. Sacco's job was to give the comic a new focus. And with the revised editorial direction came a new name: *Centrifugal Bumble-Puppy*, one he had insisted upon, but which was poorly received.

Brave New Comic

During the time Sacco decided to try his hand at editing one of Fantagraphics comic titles, he had moved back to Portland. The name change to *Centrifugal Bumble-Puppy* was actually a reference to a game played by the characters in Aldous Huxley's 1932 futuristic dystopia *Brave New World*. While Sacco thought it was an off-the-wall reference and a unique title, retailers considering *Bumble-Puppy* for the newsstands disagreed. Still, all obstacles aside, it was a chance for Sacco to make a name for himself in the world of comics, and he was up for the challenge.

His first task was to go through the abundance of existing submissions and choose the drawings that he felt would best represent his first issue. As he had done before, Sacco gravitated toward work that was political, satirical, or that raised public awareness of

The first issue of *Centrifugal Bumble-Puppy*, a humor magazine edited by Sacco beginning in 1987. Although Sacco started working for Fantagraphics as a writer, he soon found himself acting as one of the company's editors, and within a few years, a comics artist himself.

social issues. But what he ended up with were pieces that were just plain humorous. While Sacco was defining his personal choices in the world of comics, he found an absence of artists who shared his interest in using the medium to express opinions about politics or the human condition.

"I wanted [*Bumble-Puppy*] to have a social focus, and it just didn't pan out because there weren't [enough] people doing that work, especially not for the kind of money I was allowed to pay these people, which was $30 a page," Sacco said in a 1995 interview.

As its editor, Sacco offered his own brand of humor in the pages of *Bumble-Puppy*. In the third issue, its first page features a ranting manifesto about why a funny guy such as himself should compile a humor magazine at all. Apparently, *Bumble-Puppy* had received a less-than-warm reception from the masses. The same issue features a loose comic drawing of a man, presumably Sacco, speaking to a large crowd from the top of a pulpit.

Although he was its editor, he never used *Bumble-Puppy* to showcase his own comic art, which at the time had progressed. One strip from this period was included in the last few pages of *Notes*, the collection of Sacco's earlier work that was published in 2003. Under the influence of one of his favorite artists, the sixteenth-century Flemish painter Pieter Brueghel the Elder, Sacco created a masterful strip called "The Buffoon's Tale" in 1986 and 1987. Twisted and distorted faces are the hallmark of the characters, but the story itself is fantastically witty. In reading it, it becomes apparent that Sacco was on the verge of publishing his own comics, not just editing the work of other artists. Still, Sacco gave *Bumble-Puppy* everything he had.

With such a new venture, Sacco's budget remained small. More often than not, the only artists he could attract were also the ones with the least amount of experience. At the time, very few artists were creating comics about socially relevant issues. Still, *Bumble-Puppy* did expose the work of a few comics artists who would later become well known, including Tom Tomorrow and Lloyd Dangle. But while Sacco dreamed of breaking new ground with the newly directed title, its sales were thin and his editorial salary wasn't enough to pay his bills. It was around this time that he started working part-time at the public library in Portland to help make ends meet. He remembers it being at the same time that he did his first serious comic drawing, like "Voyage to the End of the Library" that appeared later in *Yahoo* number 3, and in the collected anthology *Notes*. He had taken Groth's criticism well, redirected his efforts in shorter, more satirical pieces, and began submitting them to comics like *Suburban High Life*, Robert Crumb's *Weirdo* (then edited by Crumb's wife Aline Kominsky-Crumb), and others. Finally, Sacco had found a forum for his comics, as some of this early material was now being published.

Yahoo

After a few unsuccessful issues of *Bumble-Puppy*, however, Fantagraphics killed the title in 1987, and found other work for Sacco. Around the same time, he began wondering if he could ever find an audience interested in comics that paid little reference to pop culture, but that centered instead on world affairs. He wanted to feature topics in his comics that were not commonly explored by comics artists.

Having saved some money, Sacco decided that rather than approach Groth and Thompson about another venture, he should try something on his own. He created

After several issues of *Bumble-Puppy*, Sacco decided to create a comic of his own design. Prepared to finance the printing himself, he was about to begin his career as a comics artist on his own dime, when Groth and Thompson offered to put his comic out as a Fantagraphics title. What resulted was the nine-issue comics series known as *Yahoo*, which debuted in 1988. The first issue, seen here, features Sacco's self-portrait. Drawings inside the title lettering re-create the famous 1968 photograph by Eddie Adams of General Nguyen Ngoc Loan, chief of the Vietnamese national police, shooting a Vietcong captive.

His arrangement with them was simple enough: he was permitted to follow their every move and document everything that happened while they were on their European tour. As one might expect, these activities included plenty of sex, drugs, and run-ins with the local police and customs officials. It also meant that he spent nearly every show standing behind a makeshift table selling T-shirts and other Miracle Workers memorabilia. Sacco detailed the constant complaining, partying, drinking, smoking, and meeting and losing girls by the handful. He chronicled band members' bouts with illness and visits with foreign doctors, harassment by local police, the occasional but unrelenting groupies, and the thrills of spectacular live shows. At the end of the six-week run,

In the second issue of *Yahoo*, Sacco drew inspiration from a trip he took to Europe while touring with the band the Miracle Workers. The plan was for Sacco to document everything that happened to the musicians while on the tour, which included Sacco's stint as a T-shirt vendor.

while in Berlin, Sacco bid farewell to his friends and their chaotic lifestyle. He then remained in Berlin for about five months, where he drew posters and album covers for record labels and concert promoters. During this time, he also did freelance illustration work for musicians, including the Seattle grunge outfit Mudhoney, the New Jersey indie-rock band Yo La Tengo, and the Los Angeles band Thin White Rope. He also did some record cover art for bands on the famous Seattle label, Sub Pop Records.

"How I Loved the War"

More issues of *Yahoo* followed. One in particular, *Yahoo* number 5, or "How I Loved the War," was one of Sacco's best. In it, he mixed a lively autobiographic style with a detailed chronology of the Gulf War. It was created while he was living in Berlin, breaking up with his stateside girlfriend after a failed long-distance love affair, and becoming addicted to following conflicts in the Middle East. "How I Loved the War" was one of Sacco's last auto-biographical comics. In the process of creating the issue, he began documenting his obsession in the form of a comic book. What resulted from his efforts is an intimate examination of politics from his personal viewpoint. Years later, in 2002, he said that the fifth issue of *Yahoo* remained his favorite comic book of all time since it was the one where his writing was the least restricted. He eventually hopes to return to this freeform style. By this time, fans could see that Sacco's interests were shifting. He was becoming less interested in telling his own story, and more interested in the stories of others.

In an interview with Rebecca Tuhus-Dubrow in *January Magazine*, Sacco talked about this shift in his work. "I've always been pretty political anyway, so it didn't seem like such a hop, skip, and a jump for my work to move into that sphere where autobiography [meets] politics—you can write about yourself and politics at the same time. I like that mix; I like the fact that you're not so much a participant in world events, but you're dragged along by them. That's a valid topic to write about, or as a subject for art, it's a great thing."

After a brief stay in the United States and thinning opportunities for any freelance illustration work, Sacco decided to return to Berlin in October 1990. This was about a year after Germany's reunification. The Berlin Wall, built in 1961 to limit immigration into West Germany, was erected to divide Communist East Germany and Democratic West Germany. In 1989, Germans on both sides tore down the wall. During the first anniversary of the crumbling of that once-famous symbol of Communism, Sacco was touching down in Berlin. Coincidentally, it was also his thirtieth birthday. Speaking with friends after his arrival, it was clear that not everyone was happy about Germany's reunification. Many Germans felt the process—and the adjustment that followed for its citizens on both sides of the wall—had happened too quickly. It was yet another example of how people around the world deal with and adjust to changing borders.

It was around this time that Sacco's comic style was becoming more refined. His interests turned from doing short, autobiographical pieces to longer narratives that were mostly political in scope. His most impressive work during this period was "When Good Bombs Happen to Bad People," a detailed examination of the British bombing of Germany between 1940 and 1945, the U.S. bombing of Japan between 1944 and 1945, and the U.S. bombing of Libya in 1986. By outlining the development of the decision-making process to use aerial bombing, Sacco built his narrative out of the actual speeches and broadcasts from world leaders to their citizenry. In the forward to the piece, which was reprinted in *Notes*, Sacco wrote, "Historical examples speak for themselves. In 'Good Bombs' I am letting them speak through the mouths of military men, politicians, scientists, bureaucrats, and the U.S. popular media." "Good Bombs" became a precedent-setting comic, complete with endnotes and a bibliography.

After kicking around in Germany for about a year and a half, Sacco decided to go the Middle East to see for himself the conditions of Palestine and the treatment of Palestinian refugees. He wanted to get the Palestinian point of view from the Palestinians themselves.

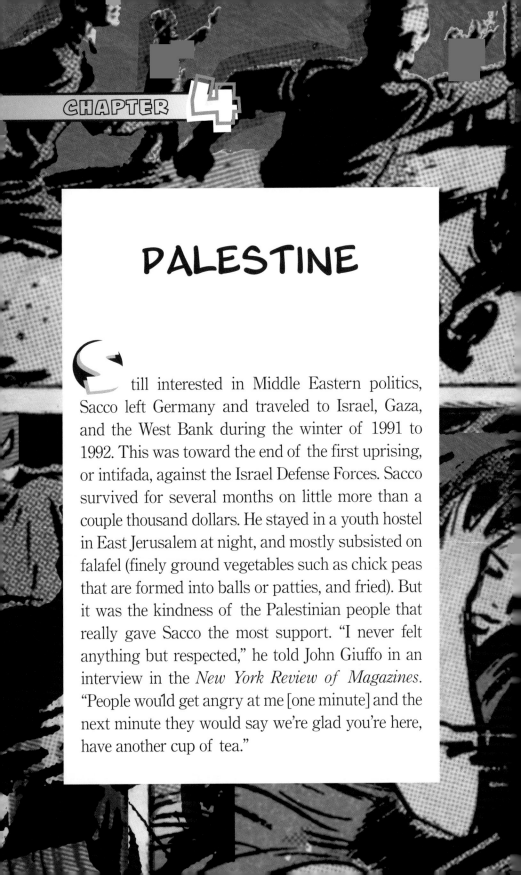

CHAPTER 4

PALESTINE

Still interested in Middle Eastern politics, Sacco left Germany and traveled to Israel, Gaza, and the West Bank during the winter of 1991 to 1992. This was toward the end of the first uprising, or intifada, against the Israel Defense Forces. Sacco survived for several months on little more than a couple thousand dollars. He stayed in a youth hostel in East Jerusalem at night, and mostly subsisted on falafel (finely ground vegetables such as chick peas that are formed into balls or patties, and fried). But it was the kindness of the Palestinian people that really gave Sacco the most support. "I never felt anything but respected," he told John Giuffo in an interview in the *New York Review of Magazines.* "People would get angry at me [one minute] and the next minute they would say we're glad you're here, have another cup of tea."

During his visit, Sacco interviewed hundreds of Palestinians in the occupied territories, chronicling the effect of the Israeli occupation of Palestine on their lives. To the Palestinians, this effect was demoralizing. Under the Israelis, they were frequently captured and sometimes tortured. Sacco explained that to the average Palestinian man, the idea of never having been imprisoned seemed like an embarrassment. If there is an unspoken solidarity among all oppressed peoples, then the Palestinians certainly share this unity.

Palestinians faced a difficult life in occupied Palestine, one with an economy controlled by Israel with few jobs, limited food and water, poor housing, and the constant threat of escalating violence. These interviews would eventually become the foundation on which Sacco built the nine individual issues of *Palestine,* a series of comics that first appeared in 1993.

For the most part, the *Palestine* series is chronological. It recounts Sacco's experiences from the minute he landed in Cairo, Egypt, to his last moments in Palestine. It also represents his first attempts at drawing more realistically. While some of the panels for *Palestine* were first done as quick sketches from direct observation, most were re-created from memory. Although Sacco brought a camera with him, he was unable to use it in many delicate situations. Sacco trained his eyes to focus on details, to remember the constant rain and mud, and the swarms of children and garbage on the graffiti-lined streets.

Sacco sarcastically compares a refugee camp in the Gaza Strip to a horrid amusement park in "Refugeeland," in an early edition of *Palestine*. Sacco documents his travels to the Middle East in notebooks and journals while traveling and then creates a narrative to illustrate upon his return home. In doing so, Sacco explains that by using repeated imagery like muddy and flooded streets, graffiti, and endless packs of children, the reader gets a unique and intimate understanding of his setting. The fifth issue of *Palestine* (inset) features Palestinians throwing rocks during the first intifada.

Clearly outraged by what he witnessed in the occupied territories, Sacco listened to anyone who revealed his or her story. In some instances, these interviews took Sacco back to 1948, shortly after the creation of Israel. At the time, thousands of Palestinians fled their towns and villages that are now part of Israel. Years later, when a few Palestinians Sacco interviewed got permission from the Israeli government to return to their homes, they found that nothing there remained the same. As one Palestinian said in *Palestine*, "There is no sign [that] we [had] ever lived there."

Sacco also spent time in Palestine's old city of Nablus, where he toured its hospital. Its two doctors were serving about 300 patients a day. Walking from bedside to bedside, each Palestinian immediately warmed to Sacco, although he was a foreigner and a Catholic. When he reached to take a photograph, each of the wounded passed to each other the *keffiyeh*, the traditional Palestinian head scarf. In a show of Arab nationalism, and with wounds worn like secret insignia, they were compelled to express their feelings of solidarity. In a later issue of *Palestine*, Sacco showed a group of Palestinians singing, "To all the people who hate us, how sweet to die for Palestine . . ."

From Nablus, Sacco headed to Balata, to see the exact sights of the first clashes of the intifada. While there, he stopped in a local school for Palestinian children, which was run with donations from the United Nations. It had no heat or electricity, and buckets caught

To get his story, Sacco toured some of the hospitals in the occupied territories, like this one in Nablus. He went from bed to bed, along with a translator, and spoke with people about their injuries, the conflict at large, and the hardships they had endured. The young girl pictured here was shot by Israeli soldiers in her schoolyard while trying to throw a stone toward them.

rainwater that dripped through a damaged roof. The volunteer educators told Sacco that while they were permitted to import Arabic texts from nearby Jordan, the Israeli government allowed only books that taught English and mathematics. Palestinian teachers were forbidden to teach history or geography, or to allow any books that showed children the history of Palestine before the creation of Israel.

Next, Sacco headed to an Israeli-built prison compound for Palestinian prisoners. He re-created in comic form its cement rooms, each 4 by 6 feet (1.2 by 1.8 meters), which sometimes held as many as thirty or forty people. Prisoners described how in ten days of captivity, they were let out only twice, each time for fifteen minutes.

This is only one threat that the Palestinians faced on a daily basis. Before long, readers of *Palestine* are informed that although the Palestinians' homes are often damaged or completely razed during the frequent raids by the Israeli army, few Palestinians are given permits to rebuild. It is because of this fact that most Palestinians are now living in illegal and substandard housing. By contrast, when an Israeli family wants to build a home in a new Israeli settlement, that family is often given an incentive grant by the government to do so. These injustices and others like them make themselves clear from page one.

But Sacco insists that his was not a completely objective portrait. He clearly is sympathetic to the Palestinian cause, and he explains this to his readers. Still, when Palestinian individuals express downright hatred toward Israeli settlers, he makes little attempt to hide their feelings. "I didn't realize the kind of antipathy some Palestinians have for Israel. It might seem obvious, but I was surprised by the level of hatred I sometimes encountered," Sacco told the *Comics Journal*. "I'm not saying that all Palestinians I met were that way; most repeated over and over that they wanted peace, but I certainly met some [who were] very hate-filled," he continued.

To help put things into perspective, Sacco also offered his readers some history, though to some, it might have been different from what was shown on the news in the United States. In Sacco's opinion, it is clear that some events in the Middle East get filtered from or softened for American audiences. He makes Israel's politics his business because, as an American tax-payer, he is also a supporter of Israel. "The United States gives Israel more money than any other country [in the world], to the tune of about $4 billion a year . . . I'm curious to see how it's spent, "Sacco said in the *Comics Journal.*

From the time he was a small boy, Sacco was con-cerned about the diaspora of people from their home country. He felt sympathetic toward people who were forced from their native land only to find themselves living in a strange place. Being in Palestine was no different. Among the thousands of refugees, who had lost their homes to the Israeli settlements, there was solidarity, a unity forged by suffering.

Readers of the comic series (and later book) *Palestine* are immediately captivated by Sacco's intimate descrip-tions of the horrifying and relentless humiliation of the Palestinians at the hands of Israeli soldiers. Threatened by a constant curfew, changing rules, roadblocks, ques-tioning, and frequent arrests, the Palestinians are eager to tell their story. They take Sacco by the hand and share with him cup after cup of sugar-laden tea and their recent scars, reminders of bullets shot by an occupying army in an occupied land.

Sacco's story, a recounting of events during the first Palestinian intifada that took place beginning in December 1987, mostly takes place in a refugee camp in Gaza known

In one of the most powerful sequences in *Palestine*, Sacco tells the story of a man being held in an Israeli prison camp for several days. In the panels that follow, the squares repeat themselves over several pages as a suggestion of his oppression and how time in custody is passing very slowly. The last image in the story, by contrast, is a half-page illustration that reveals the man's joyousness at being released.

as Jabalia. At the time, the Palestinians had been living under the Israeli occupation for more than twenty years, and they were angry enough to rise up against them. Actions by Palestinians had become more violent. Throwing rocks, Molotov cocktails, and hand grenades at Israeli soldiers occurred more often. After four Palestinians died during the insurgency in Jabalia, the violence spread to the rest of Gaza and then into the West Bank. The first intifada ended in 1993, after more than 1,000 Palestinians were killed and 20,000 others were injured. During the same period, and in the years that followed, Israelis suffered losses, too, with some estimates claiming that more than 100 were killed while countless others were injured. During the first intifada, Israelis razed thousands of Palestinian homes, readying the ground for settlements. In some cases, the foundations are still visible.

In other segments in the book, Sacco tells the story of Palestinians who were shot dead just for peering from the terrace of their apartment building. While one family member died instantly, the other slowly bled to death over the course of several hours. The Israeli-imposed curfew wouldn't allow the victim's family to transport him to the already over-burdened hospital. The Israeli soldier responsible for the deaths was released the same day he went to court. And the atrocities continued.

Arab-Israeli Relations

Since 1917 and the end of World War I, the question of who has the right to live in Palestine has been an issue between nations. With the disintegration of the Turkish Ottoman Empire during the early part of the twentieth century, Palestine had fallen under the control of Great Britain. While most of the former Turkish territories had become independent countries, Palestine was an exception. It was instead considered a mandated territory, meaning that the control of Palestine (and who could live on its soil) was to be determined by the British government. In doing so, the British issued what became known as the Balfour Declaration, which expressed support for Palestine being the national home of the Jewish people. Under these new guidelines, those of the Palestine Mandate (1922–1947), many European Jews immigrated into Palestine where they made their home. This immigration swelled even further after World War II, since Jews from all over Europe fled Nazi persecution. By 1937, in response to the large Jewish immigration into Palestine, Arabs there demanded that Palestine become an independent Arab state. When their call went unheard by the British, they reacted to the steady influx of Jews into Palestine with rebellion. When attempts by Great Britain to quell the violence brought little results, representatives from the United Nations were asked to address this violent relationship between Arabs and Jews.

The Creation of Israel

In 1947, the United Nations proposed dividing Palestine into two independent states: one where Palestinian

Arabs could reside without fear of being pushed from their homes, and one where Jews could live in peace without reprisal from Arabs who feared losing their homeland. The holy city of Jerusalem, important to both those who practice Islam and Judaism, was to remain under international control. This partition plan, which was unsuccessful, gave rise instead to the independent state of Israel in 1948, formerly the proposed "Jewish" section of Palestine. But problems between the two groups worsened even after the creation of Israel.

Israel expanded its territory during the first war between the Arabs and Israelis after Israel was invaded by Arab forces from Egypt, Syria, Jordan, Lebanon, and Iraq in 1948. At this time, Israeli soldiers began occupying Arab Palestine, and by the end of the conflict, they had absorbed 77 percent of Palestine into Israel, creating Israeli-occupied Palestine. Israelis had also absorbed the larger section of Jerusalem during this period. Due to this expansion of Israel into Arab lands, more than half of the indigenous Palestinians fled their homeland willingly or were expelled by force. Soon Jordan and Egypt occupied the remaining Palestinian territory, once slated to become an independent Palestinian state under the 1947 United Nations proposal. Fighting between Israelis and Arabs continued. While some 800,000 Arabs once lived in the area that became Israel after 1948, only 170,000 remained, ending the Arab majority in the Jewish state.

The 1956 War

Although a truce, issued by the United Nations, was put in place in 1949, fighting between Arabs and Israelis continued. The nationalization of Egypt's Suez Canal in 1956 further aggravated these already tenuous relationships, and tensions between Arabs and Israelis again resulted in war in 1956. Although the United Nations installed a cease-fire agreement within days, Israel continued to occupy Gaza until 1957.

During the early part of the 1960s, tensions in the Arab world increased as border incidents between Syria, Egypt, Jordan, and Israel intensified. (Palestinians were often supported by Syrian troops.) And while Egypt's president Gamal Nasser tried to settle the violence by mobilizing Egyptian troops in the Sinai and closing the Gulf of Aqaba to Israel, his attempts failed. Soon the Israelis responded with force. It was also around this time that the Arabs organized the Palestine Liberation Organization, or PLO.

The 1967 War

In the spring of 1967, violence by Palestinian groups increased. By June, these tensions erupted into an all-out war between Arabs and Israelis over the Palestinian territory now controlled by Jordan and Egypt. Israel gained the upper hand in the 1967 war (known as the Six-Day War) and gained total control over the Sinai Peninsula including the West Bank, the Gaza Strip, and the highly sought-after territory known as the Golan Heights. This portion of Palestine also included the remainder of Arab East Jerusalem, which was subsequently annexed by Israel. The conflict, which ended on June 10, 1967, proved the superiority of the Israeli air and ground forces.

More Palestinians fled the region by the thousands, though later estimates claimed that the new occupation gave rise to the displacement of half a million Palestinian Arabs in 1967 alone. By November 22 of that same year, the United Nations issued Security Council Resolution 242, calling on Israel to withdraw from the Palestinian territories it had occupied in the 1967 war, but it had little effect. Arabs and Israelis continually attacked one another during this period, especially in the occupied areas.

The Invasion of Lebanon

Eventually, low-level violence between Arabs and Israelis erupted into another war in 1973. This conflict was purposefully instigated by Egypt's president Anwar Sadat beginning on October 6, the Jewish holy day of Yom Kippur. Fighting by Egyptian Arabs was fierce, and the Israel Defense Forces suffered severe casualties. By November, Egypt and Israel signed a cease-fire agreement and swapped prisoners of war. Peace agreements between the two nations were established in January 1974 that called for Israel to withdraw from Sinai. In turn, Egypt agreed to affirm Israel's right to exist. In 1979, the two nations established diplomatic relations under the Camp David Accords. But Israel's withdraw from Sinai was slow, further aggravating neighboring Arabs.

In the early 1980s, after the last of the Israeli forces were leaving Sinai, violence began again. Israel invaded Beirut, Lebanon, and bombed an apartment building, killing 300 civilians in July 1981. A full-scale invasion of

In this photograph by Françoise de Mulder, an elderly man stands alongside the ruins of houses in Beirut following the Israeli invasion of Lebanon in 1982. Although the invasion lasted less than two weeks, the Israelis, the Palestinians, and the Syrians in Lebanon inflicted heavy casualties. The catalyst for the invasion was the assassination attempt of Israeli ambassador Shlomo Argov in London and the buildup of the PLO in south Lebanon.

Lebanon by Israeli forces followed in 1982. Thousands died in Lebanon during the fighting, with some estimates by the International Red Cross approximating the combined total of Israelis, Lebanese, and Palestinian deaths at more than 62,000 between 1982 and 1987. Finally, in 2000, Israel completely left Lebanon. Within a few years of the 1982 invasion, however, violence erupted again as rioting broke out in the Israeli-occupied territories of Gaza, the

West Bank, and Jerusalem. Eventually, the uprising on the part of the Arabs living in those areas became known as the first intifada.

The surge of violence by Arabs in the 1987 intifada, brought on by the Israeli occupation of Arab

The Palestinian fighter seen in this 1988 photograph taken in the West Bank holds a large stone presumably because he is about to cast it toward Israeli soldiers during the first intifada, or Palestinian uprising (1987–1993). Many Palestinian civilians took up the fight against the Israelis during the uprising by throwing stones, axes, hand grenades, and Molotov cocktails, or glass bottles filled with flammable liquids and sealed with a rag that is set on fire.

land, was eventually calmed with talk of the 1993
Oslo Accords, which promised to recognize some
form of Palestinian self-government in the West
Bank and Gaza before 1995. The Oslo Accords were
somewhat successful in the 1990s at keeping violence
at bay, but they have ultimately led to a stalemate.
The agreement offered Palestinians a chance at
achieving independence, the partial withdrawal of
Israeli forces from Arab lands, and the election of the
Palestinian council, but further attempts to finalize
these steps toward Palestinian sovereignty have ultimately failed.

Back in the United States

Sacco left the hostel in East Jerusalem in 1992 and
headed back to the United States, back to Portland,
where he began drawing what would eventually
become the first *Palestine* comic. At this point, his
expressive drawing style had matured. Sacco's work
was easily identifiable by its unusual angles and
dense cross-hatching, which increased the three-
dimensional look of the war-torn landscapes and
brought life to the faces in the portraits of weathered
Palestinians. Highly detailed images swept dramati-
cally across entire pages of *Palestine*, and its panels
were divided in a great variety of methods and sizes.
Some of these divisions were masterful for helping
the viewer participate in the emotional stories. For
instance, when one Palestinian victim is being held in
prison, the panels shrink with each passing day,

denoting the slow, painful passage of time and the growing oppression felt by the detained man. In another example, the final panel of a series that shows a Palestinian victim being beaten fades to black when he reaches a state of unconsciousness.

In Sacco's control, the comics medium is a surprisingly perfect way to introduce new readers and even seasoned ones to tragedies, both great and small. His economy of words and images flawlessly re-creates war-torn territories in the simplest terms, with the simplest language. But the process of creating his nonfiction works is hardly a simple one. Sacco has since stated that it takes up to three days to draw one page, and this is only after he has gone through hundreds of notebooks filled with observations, interviews, and anecdotes, whittling them down to a workable narrative.

Creating *Palestine* took several years throughout the early 1990s. While he was working on the series, he took on shorter freelance work for other comics, namely profiles of several well-known jazz musicians for Harvey Pekar's *American Splendor*, as well as stories for several comics anthologies including short pieces for *Real Stuff* and *Buzzard*. Later projects included the *Big Book of Martyrs* (Factoid Books) and a written introduction to a book of Eric Drooker's called *Blood Song: A Silent Ballad* (Harvest Books). This was also around the same time that Fantagraphics released some of Sacco's early collected comics in *Spotlight on the Genius That Is Joe Sacco* and *War Junkie*, which compiled work that previously appeared in *Yahoo* and in an anthology from the Canadian comics publisher Drawn & Quarterly.

Despite *Palestine*'s visual artistry and careful, honest depiction of the subject matter, its early sales were poor. It seemed as though few comics readers were interested in learning about events in the Middle East. When the second issue followed, its sales faired no better. At this point Sacco was disappointed, but he continued working. It would be years before *Palestine* found its larger audience.

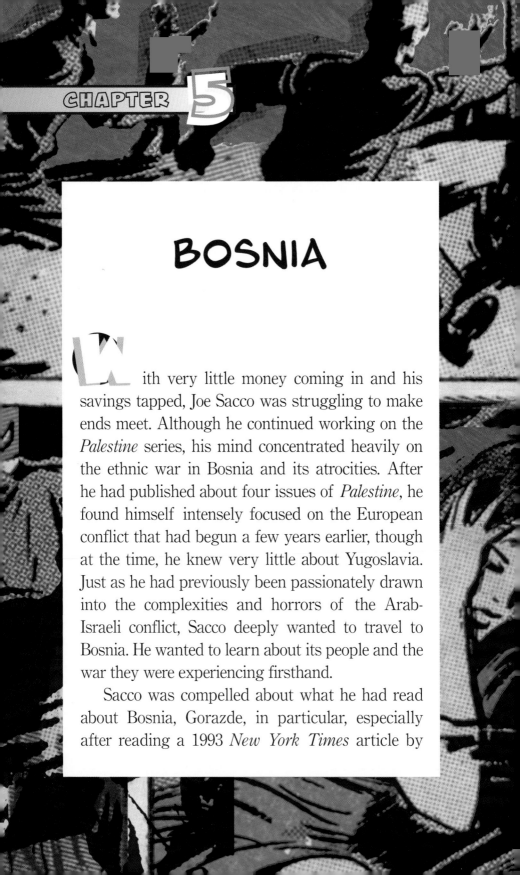

CHAPTER 5

BOSNIA

With very little money coming in and his savings tapped, Joe Sacco was struggling to make ends meet. Although he continued working on the *Palestine* series, his mind concentrated heavily on the ethnic war in Bosnia and its atrocities. After he had published about four issues of *Palestine*, he found himself intensely focused on the European conflict that had begun a few years earlier, though at the time, he knew very little about Yugoslavia. Just as he had previously been passionately drawn into the complexities and horrors of the Arab-Israeli conflict, Sacco deeply wanted to travel to Bosnia. He wanted to learn about its people and the war they were experiencing firsthand.

Sacco was compelled about what he had read about Bosnia, Gorazde, in particular, especially after reading a 1993 *New York Times* article by

John Burns, a journalist who had slipped into the town through Serbian lines. In an interview for the arts program *EGG*, Sacco told of his desire to travel there.

"About the time I was halfway through the *Palestine* series, I started to become a little interested in what was going on in the Balkans. The war had started a couple of years before. I didn't understand the whole . . . situation, like a lot of people. In the same way that Palestine started to pull me in, the same thing happened [with Bosnia]. I became outraged with what was going on. I was basically disgusted with American policy and I thought there should be an intervention." With his mind racing, Sacco started tracing the complex history of the Yugoslavian people. Before long, he knew that he had to get to Bosnia.

A History of Yugoslavia

The Kingdom of Yugoslavia was divided after World War II in 1946 by the Communist leader Josip Broz Tito (commonly known as Tito) into six republics: Bosnia-Herzegovina, Croatia, Macedonia, Montenegro, Serbia, and Slovenia. Under Tito, who was president of the entire Socialist Federal Republic of Yugoslavia until his death in 1980, life in the republic was civil and prosperous. People of all nationalities and religions lived side by side.

After Tito's death in 1980, ethnic tensions developed throughout the republics, beginning in Croatia. Soon Communist leader Slobodan Milosevic gained Serbian support when he started speaking about Serbian nationalism. In doing so, all of the other ethnic groups in the republic were isolated by the Serbs. Milosevic instituted a policy of "one person, one vote" for the Serbs, who at the time comprised a majority in the republic. The fall of Communism in the Soviet Union and in Eastern Europe further complicated matters in Yugoslavia, which was politically unstable. Each of the republics began electing a new form of government. Slovenia and Croatia, for instance, favored independence, while Serbia and Montenegro wanted to remain part of a union of republics.

In 1990, the Yugoslav People's Army met with the Presidency of Yugoslavia (at the time an eight-member council) in an attempt to impose martial law over the entire republic, but no plan could be agreed upon. Before long, the republics hungry for sovereignty moved past the idea of unity. Slovenia and Croatia declared independence in 1991, and Macedonia and Bosnia-Herzegovina followed a year later. When Communist leader Milosevic and the Yugoslav People's Army tried to prevent the new states from separating from the republic, the ghastly Yugoslav Wars began, killing an estimated 100,000 to 300,000 people between 1992 and 1995.

As Sacco revealed in his book *Safe Area Gorazde*, the genocide that existed in the republics of Yugoslavia in the 1990s did not originate in the brutality between the Serbs and Croats during WWII, but by the later propaganda of Milosevic and his push toward Serbian

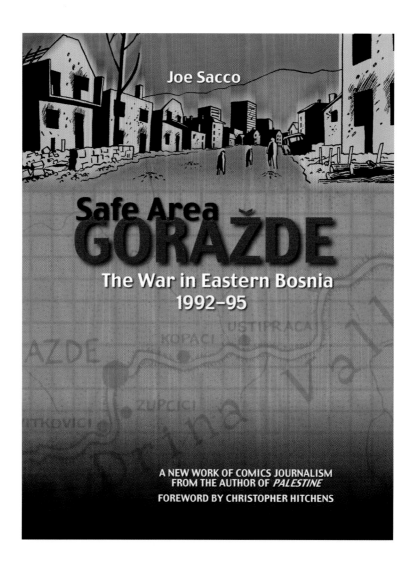

Safe Area
GORAŽDE
The War in Eastern Bosnia
1992–95

Joe Sacco

A NEW WORK OF COMICS JOURNALISM
FROM THE AUTHOR OF *PALESTINE*
FOREWORD BY CHRISTOPHER HITCHENS

In 1995, Sacco headed into eastern Bosnia to learn firsthand about the ethnic war in Yugoslavia between the Serbs and Muslims. He lived for several months with a Muslim family in a United Nations designated "safe area" known as Gorazde, a Muslim enclave that was virtually cut off from the rest of the world. Published in 2000, *Safe Area Gorazde: The War in Eastern Bosnia 1992–95* immediately resonated with readers and critics alike and earned Sacco a permanent role as a respected American journalist.

nationalism. Sacco carefully and successfully explained the ethnic and religious differences between the groups and explored the reasons behind the violence while retelling the story of Gorazde and its people. Milosevic was later arrested and tried for his crimes of political abuse and corruption in 2001. His trial for charges of genocide began a year later and is still ongoing at the time of this writing. If convicted of war crimes, Milosevic could be sentenced to life in prison.

The Road to Bosnia

Before Sacco could even think about going to Bosnia, he had to finish the last issue of *Palestine*, which he did in 1995. A year earlier, while living in Portland, he had met a poet at a party who had been to Bosnia, so Sacco questioned him thoroughly about what steps he would need to make. Sacco found out that in order to go to Bosnia as a freelance reporter, he would need a letter from a publisher stating that he or she would buy his work. With this in mind, he flew to New York. Although he was given the letter as a personal favor, Sacco was now one step closer to going to Bosnia.

Knowing he would eventually be heading to the Balkans, Sacco then traveled back to Germany where he further prepared for his trip while staying with friends. To make the journey, he needed to obtain a United Nations press card, which was difficult to get. On top of this, he suspected that if he was evaluated on the basis of his work as a cartoonist, the UN representatives would never permit him to make the

PRESSTION

Nº 14658

: accredited
ease extend
iecessary to

ALSO VALID IFOR

Nations Peace F
orces - Impleme
ntation Forces -
- United Nations
ations Peace Fo
orces - Implemer
ntation Forces - I
- United Nations
ations Peace For
orces - Implemen
ntation Forces - t
- United Nations I
ations Peace Fort
orces - Implement
ntation Forces - U
- United Nations P
ations Peace Forc
orces - Implementa
ntation Forces - Un
- United Nations Pt
ations Peace Force
orces - Implementat
ntation F

UNITED NATIONS
PEACE FORCES

Name: JOSEPH SACCO
Signature: *Joseph Sacco*
News agency: FOUR WALLS 8 WINDOWS
Authorized by: S. O'cent
Issuing Office: ZAGREB
Issue date: 20.12.95   Exp: 31.1.96

In December 1996, with a letter in hand explaining that he was writing for the publisher Four Walls and Eight Windows, Sacco obtained this United Nations press card in Croatia in order to head into Gorazde, then an isolated Muslim enclave. Feeling panicked that his earlier work as a comics journalist would be poorly received by UN officials, he was relieved to find that they didn't even question his past experience.

trip. As luck would have it, however, his work was never examined.

In a 2001 interview with Gary Groth, founder of Fantagraphics, Sacco explained the process. "I took the train, I went to Zagreb [Croatia], and I found out where the United Nations had its headquarters, went to the press officer in this little container. It was basically one of those containers that are made into offices. And it was filled with other journalists, like I think a Spanish crew and a Canadian [television] crew, about eight or nine people just demanding to get back to Sarajevo. Their credentials had expired. They wanted their papers. They had to get there [that night]. They were just banging on a table making a noise. I just gave the press officer my application, my photographs, and my passport and I didn't say a word. They didn't say a word to me. They just wanted somebody out of there. Within ten minutes, I had the press card. I didn't talk to anyone. I didn't show my book to anyone. I thought, 'Thank God. God is with me on this.'"

Although Sacco had nearly everything he needed to make the journey to Sarajevo, he had no idea how to get there. At the time, airplanes were being fired upon, so his only choice was to go by land. He was told to find another journalist and go along with him or her, but this also proved difficult. Then he found that the United Nations was allowing journalists to ride along with their convoys. (The United Nations was bringing much needed food, water, and medical supplies into the region.) UN officials then told Sacco that he would need more gear.

With his coveted UN press card in hand, Sacco had all but one item that he needed to make the difficult journey—a flak jacket. But not being able to afford the expensive life-saving gear in Croatia, where he was at the time, he was forced to take a bus back to Munich, Germany, to special order the item. Although he was told that he couldn't go to Sarajevo without it, when he finally made the decision to grab the next UN convoy, no other journalists wore the heavy, bulletproof vest. As usual, the entire process had been one great learning experience.

GO AWAY

No-man's-land

nearing Gorazde

In the fall of 1995, the future of Gorazde and its 57,000 inhabitants was by no means clear...

Gorazde's Blue Road, the only way in and out of the Muslim enclave while Sacco was a journalist there in 1995, quickly becomes a metaphor in *Safe Area Gorazde* since it symbolized both isolation and freedom for Gorazde's remaining residents. During his mosaic of a story, Sacco frequently felt guilty since he was able to come and go via the Blue Road while his friends in Gorazde were forced to stay behind despite their desire to escape.

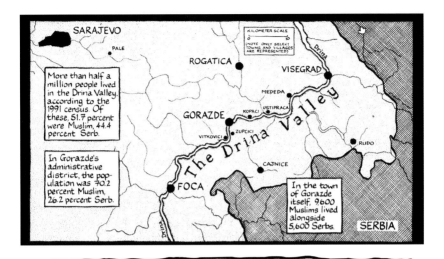

This map of the Drina Valley in Yugoslavia was featured in Sacco's Safe Area Gorazde to help readers visualize the area in which Sacco was referring while writing about residents in the Muslim enclave. According to Sacco's research, more than half a million people (about 52 percent Muslim and 44 percent Serbian) lived in the Drina Valley before the conflict.

Safe Area Gorazde

Sacco arrived in Sarajevo in the fall of 1995, on the back of a UN convoy. After spending about six weeks in Bosnia's capital city, which he said was inundated by foreign news correspondents, he ended up in Gorazde, a UN designated "safe area," and an enclave surrounded by separatist Serbian forces. The United Nations had recently finished a bombing campaign against Serbian forces in that area, but under the terms of the cease-fire agreement, UN convoys were now permitted to enter the region.

Gorazde is a small town located in eastern Bosnia in the heart of the Drina Valley. At the time of Sacco's arrival in 1995, three and a half years into the war, its population was about 57,000 people, most of them Muslims. (The other two UN designated safe areas—Srebrenica and Zepa—were recently abandoned by the United Nations after they were invaded by Serbian forces. In other words, Gorazde was far from being a safe place.)

In his book, Sacco explained the history behind the breakup of Yugoslavia and how, prior to the war, Serbs, who are primarily Orthodox Christians, and Muslims had lived beside one another in harmony for years after World War II. He then explained how nationalist leaders had exploited the worries and speculations of the Serbs to the point that they were fearful enough to retaliate on their Muslim friends and neighbors, people whom they had known and lived beside for their entire lives. Sacco soon realized just how susceptible people are to political propaganda, as even he claimed to have demonized the Serbs prior to his firsthand experiences in Bosnia. He told Groth, "[Before I went to Bosnia] my political preconceptions were that a war was being fought against a people [who] were trying to keep a multiethnic society together. [After my arrival] my perception of who the Serbs were was mitigated by actually crossing the lines and meeting them. I must say that I still feel that they were heavily propagandized. I still heard hateful things coming out of their mouths that I didn't hear on the other side of the lines. I mean, it seemed as though even educated people had swallowed the propaganda of the state. It was very distressing."

The next night, Riki invited Edin, Whit, a Turkish journalist named Serif, and me to his home for dinner. Riki's mother served pots of coffee and wave after wave of Bosnian specialties, indulging us in a way that was extravagant then and would have been impossible just two weeks before...

Afterwards, Riki ran through every Beatles, Doors and Stones song he knew, and some he didn't. He reprised 'Hotel California' two or three times...

THIS COULD BE HEAVEN OR THIS COULD BE HELL

In this panel from *Safe Area Gorazde*, Sacco joins some of his friends for an evening of discussion and entertainment. Clockwise from left is Sacco, followed by Edin, one of the central characters in the book and in whose home Sacco lived during his stay in Gorazde, Edin's friend Riki, a Bosnian soldier who spends much of the book playing his guitar and singing American rock songs before heading back to the front, Riki's friend Whit, and a Turkish journalist named Serif. Sacco has attributed his success in journalism to his ability to spend a great deal of time with people during times of strife rather than being forced to work on extremely tight deadlines like most other writers must.

As soon as he arrived in Gorazde, Sacco felt an immediate connection to the small town and its courageous people. He was living with his friend Edin, Edin's parents, and Edin's brother in a bombed out home that, after repairs, had several rebuilt rooms. Sacco wrote, "Every morning, before tending to the animals, Edin's mom would tiptoe into the room where I slept to get the wood fire going in the stove. Water was boiled and dinner was heated on the stove. Clothes were dried above it. The stove provided the house's only heat. I loved that stove."

Sacco wondered how Gorazde's citizens had managed to survive without adequate water, food, shelter, medical supplies, and electricity, while so many were in hiding. During his first few days, he, along with his new friends, were waiting for news to come about the end of the war. People were happy and hopeful, though it was apparent that the atrocities of the last few years had ultimately taken their toll on everyone. Every now and then, something seemingly tolerable, such as the swelling of hands due to washing clothes in the cold Drina River, caused Edin's mother to burst into hysterics. Sacco realized that these were a people who had been pushed to their limits.

During his stay in Gorazde, Sacco learned that the violence and hate were largely spread by one group of Serbs—the Chetniks—though not all Serbs were part of this group. Other Serbs followed in the bloody frenzy, urged in part by propaganda. Slowly, in discussions with his characters in his book, Sacco got the remaining residents of Gorazde to tell their stories and ask themselves painful questions. What resulted is a desperate and moving plea. One evening, Sabina, one of Sacco's new friends, asks, "Do Americans know about what's going on in Gorazde?" Reluctantly, Sacco answered that they do.

Days and days passed and no news of the end of the war came. Still, Gorazde's remaining Muslim residents seemed happy and thankful for the recent deliveries of flour and beans, and bandages and blood supplies. Juice and bread were plentiful, at least for now. Meanwhile, whispers of Serbs could be heard as close as the nearby Drina River, still cold with the blood of hundreds of dumped Muslim bodies, men, women, and children whose throats were savagely cut by Serbs. Sacco recounted one soldier's story, a man named Rasim, of witnessing these horrible murders in the name of ethnic cleansing.

"I was an eyewitness when the Chetniks brought two families—both families had three kids—and killed them behind the bridge. They cut their throats and pushed them into the river . . . the Guso and Sabanovic families. First they killed the children . . . And I was an eyewitness when a Chetnik cut off the breast of one of the mothers who was trying to protect her kids."

Sacco introduced his readers to Gorazde's few doctors, who had kept the hospital functional without electricity or even clean water. They had no anesthetics and no painkillers, and were forced to perform all types of surgical procedures without the aid of anything but, at times, a kitchen knife and a bit of alcohol to dull the pain. Overall, *Safe Area Gorazde* is both a moving story of the betrayal of a people and a tribute to their courageous survival.

While page after page of the book recounted similar horrors, Sacco kept his book from being a catalog of atrocities. Most of the graphic brutality is shown as flashbacks, interspersed with a much-needed history of Yugoslavia, as well as plenty of interaction between himself and his new friends. Through it all, Sacco felt a sense of guilt because he could leave the enclave through the one and only Blue Road, while his friends,

These graphic and violent images of Muslims getting their throats cut and their dead bodies being throw over the side of a bridge in Gorazde help illustrate the information as it is told to Sacco by Rasim, who witnessed the murders. In proceeding panels, Sacco describes the fact that the man overheard Serbian soldiers saying to their Muslim prisoners who were taken from their homes in the middle of the night, "You don't need shoes. You're going to be killed in a few minutes."

desperate for anything new—news from the outside world, American films and fashion, even a new magazine—are stuck inside the Muslim enclave. Sacco even brought magazines to the local library and knock-off Levi's 501s to a few friends, and delivered plenty of letters and packages from loved ones back in Sarajevo. Eventually, Sacco made three trips to Bosnia in the mid-1990s, and he remains in contact with many of the people he met from the region.

When he finally returned to Portland, Sacco found that sales of *Palestine* were increasing, and the series, then published as a book, had been well received, so well received, in fact, that it earned him a 1996 American Book Award. Finally it seemed as though Sacco was getting both the credit and support that he needed to keep writing and drawing.

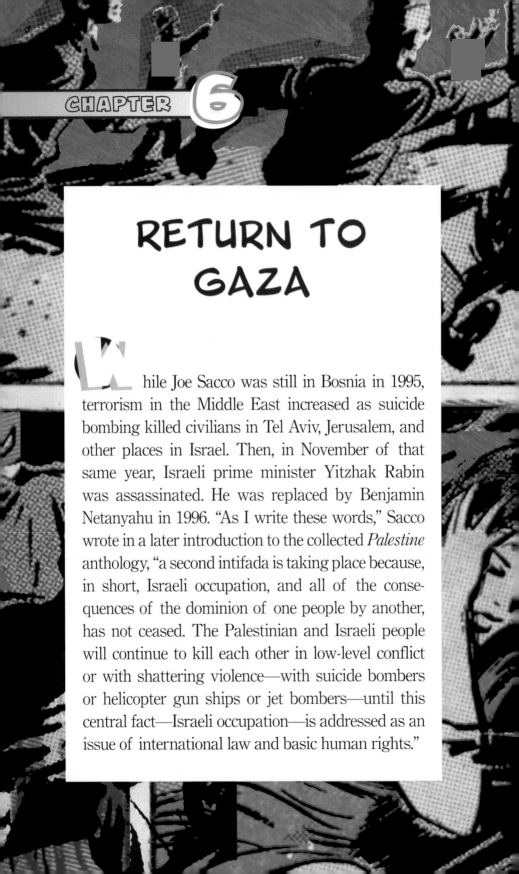

CHAPTER 6

RETURN TO GAZA

While Joe Sacco was still in Bosnia in 1995, terrorism in the Middle East increased as suicide bombing killed civilians in Tel Aviv, Jerusalem, and other places in Israel. Then, in November of that same year, Israeli prime minister Yitzhak Rabin was assassinated. He was replaced by Benjamin Netanyahu in 1996. "As I write these words," Sacco wrote in a later introduction to the collected *Palestine* anthology, "a second intifada is taking place because, in short, Israeli occupation, and all of the consequences of the dominion of one people by another, has not ceased. The Palestinian and Israeli people will continue to kill each other in low-level conflict or with shattering violence—with suicide bombers or helicopter gun ships or jet bombers—until this central fact—Israeli occupation—is addressed as an issue of international law and basic human rights."

At the end of 1996, Israel announced its plans to expand Jewish settlements, which outraged Palestinians. The year 1999 brought another attempt at peace with the Wye River Accord and the first open "safe passage" between the West Bank and the Gaza Strip. However, Palestinian and Israeli negotiations again failed to finalize border agreements. Many Palestinians felt that because so much time had passed without a successful compromise between the two groups, the earlier Oslo Accords were void.

War Crimes

In 1998, Sacco's attentions returned to the war in Bosnia, and he flew to the Netherlands to cover the UN's Bosnian war crimes trial from the Hague. His 1998 article in *Details*, "The War Crimes Trials," detailed the tribunal in general, and a few criminal investigations. He landed the job with the help of Art Spiegelman, of *Maus* fame, who was then *Details* comix editor at large. In the article, Sacco wrote, "At least someone somewhere is drawing the line—if only a legal line—on carnage as we stumble out of this century of horrors." The six-page piece has been called the magazine's best work of journalism to date. Two other short pieces further explored Sacco's experiences in the Balkans: "Christmas with Karadzic," a misadventure that appeared in a 1997 comic anthology called *Zero Zero*, and a forty-one-page comic about people he met in Sarajevo published by Drawn & Quarterly called *Soba*, which was released in 1998.

Meanwhile, Sacco was following the position of the Clinton administration and its stance toward the Arab-Israeli conflict, one that he viewed as being overtly pro-Israel. That same year, President Bill Clinton managed to convene a summit meeting between PLO chairman Yasser Arafat and then-Israeli prime minister Ehud Barak in 2000. Although some talk was made about moving Oslo negotiations forward, no additional resolutions were made. The meeting between the two leaders was considered a failure, a move, some suggested, made exclusively for political reasons to gain the attention of the world press. The Palestinians were outraged. In response, they organized a second intifada, and violence steadily escalated on both sides. Palestinian suicide bombers began attacking Israelis more often, and any talks of peace between the two groups became unlikely. As a result of this new uprising, the Israel Defense Forces reoccupied the West Bank.

Life Among the Ruins

Between 2000 and 2002, Sacco took several trips back to both Bosnia and Hebron, in the West Bank. Despite the multiple attempts at peace agreements between the Arabs and the Israelis, he estimated that the fighting between them had worsened. During the summer of 2001, he traveled to Gaza, where he visited (and stayed in) Khan Younis, a Palestinian refugee camp in Rafah, on the southern border of Gaza. The accommodations allowed him more of an insider's view of the Arab struggle to survive.

"I felt that I was much more on the inside this time," Sacco told *January Magazine*. "[The occupied territories] seemed a lot harder, a lot more violent. There were a lot of house demolitions going on there, and there are just some spooky parts of town because they're basically under fire, or in zones where there are a lot of bullets flying around at different times."

Because Sacco wanted to experience life as a refugee, he wanted to remain in Rafah for as long as possible. He wanted a chance to meet people and get to know their specific circumstances. He wanted to befriend Palestinians, to hear their intimate stories in order to depict them as they actually are.

Getting to the camp, however, was nearly impossible. Sacco recalled all of the Israeli checkpoints during his journey and how, at times, a person could be stopped for hours or even days at any one spot for questioning. Other times, the Israel Defense Forces entirely closed the one road into Rafah. During his first trip, his travel was less restricted and taxis were available for the asking. Now staying in a refugee camp, his visit was much different; Rafah was more remote and inaccessible.

New York

When Sacco returned from Gaza in 2001, he moved from Portland to New York, where he crashed on a friend's couch in Brooklyn. By day, he sought freelance work with national magazines, and during the evenings, he searched for a place to live. Eventually, he found an apartment share in Queens in 2001.

In this detailed drawing, Sacco shows his readers an unlikely perspective of the Khan Younis Palestinian refugee camp. Conditions in the camp were horrible, and its residents were often forced to use any available materials to rebuild the tiny cinder block structures with makeshift corrugated metal roofs. This remarkable illustration was printed in "A Gaza Diary: Scenes from the Palestinian Uprising," an article by Middle East reporter Chris Hedges for a collaborative piece with Sacco in 2001 for *Harper's* magazine.

Sacco's work has since appeared in such high-profile magazines as *Harper's*, which in October 2001, used his drawings of Rafah to illustrate a piece by Chris Hedges, a friend of Sacco's and a reporter for the *New York Times*, as well as in *Time* magazine. Around the same time, Sacco began a short stint as a teacher at one of New York's most popular art schools, the School of Visual Arts.

Other freelance projects followed too, such as a 2001 project for the New Press. Sacco was asked to illustrate a book by Priscilla Murolo on the history of the U.S. labor movement called *From the Folks Who Brought You the Weekend: A Short Illustrated History of Labor in the United States*. Again, he would use his immense talent for drawing to bring life—and humor—to historical subject matter. The combination of hand-drawn illustrations with politics and issues surrounding the labor movement was not new. The Industrial Workers of the World—nick-named the Wobblies—often used cartoons to get their message to the masses in the early 1900s.

Even with the work pouring in, Sacco felt his life in New York was unsettled. The pace of the city was too frenzied, and it became difficult for him to stick to a rigid drawing schedule. In his short time on the East Coast, Sacco found that the city that never sleeps was just too distracting. With money steadily coming in, he finally decided to look for a more permanent place to live. In 2003, Sacco returned to his beloved Portland, where he settled in a rambling old house in the southwest section of the city. He proudly boasted about buying a 1950s-style couch (for him, a sign of permanent residency) and has most of his art and his comics collection in one city. In the rear of his new place, he was finally able to listen to his blues/jazz collection while writing and drawing comics underneath an oversized window.

The year 2003 also saw the release of another graphic novel (a term that Sacco loathes, for his works are all nonfiction, not typical "novels") that was generated out of research culled from Sacco's numerous trips to Bosnia. In *The Fixer: A Story from Sarajevo*, Sacco profiles the life of Neven, a "fixer" who helped journalists mix with the local scene in Sarajevo and got them the contacts they might need to get their stories. In *The Fixer*, Sacco returns to Bosnia during the last days of the war and explores Neven's lifestyle and past as a sniper who sought to exploit whatever he could out of the conflict. Although Sacco returned to Bosnia several times between 2000 and 2001, he kept following the unease in the Middle East. Events in Gaza kept him from going back to the region, and by February 2003, he headed back there again to conduct more research, perhaps for an upcoming comic book. He took yet another trip to the region in May of that same year.

"It bothers me that people are suffering in Gaza," he told James Adams of www.globeandmail.com. "And I want it to bother other people, too. It's as simple as that."

President George W. Bush's agenda for bringing peace to both the Palestinians and the Israelis, the Road Map to Peace, was also announced in 2003. In an attempt to install a complete cease-fire agreement between the two sides, the Mideast Quartet (the United States, the European Union, Russia, and the United Nations) formulated the negotiations.

This panel is part of a collection of strips that Sacco drew for *From the Folks Who Brought You the Weekend: A Short Illustrated History of Labor in the United States*, a book published by the New Press in 2001. Although the book was written by Priscilla Murolo and A. B. Chitty, Sacco provided a series of powerful illustrations, most offering a pictorial history of the U.S. labor movement from the workers' perspective. In this panel, Sacco is seen as a once-powerful and arrogant CEO whose job has been eliminated due to corporate downsizing. In the last box, Sacco, now a janitor, is chided by another worker who tells him that other janitors in Los Angeles have formed a union for better pay and benefits, a move he previously criticized as a CEO.

Sacco, still doubtful that the conflict will be settled, wrote about his recent experiences in Rafah in a piece for the *New York Times Magazine* in July 2003. In it he explained the significance of Rafah, from both the Palestinian and Israeli points of view. At the time, and during the previous year, more than 860 houses had been destroyed in one stretch of land there, Sacco estimated. But the Israelis insisted that most of the destroyed homes were uninhabited. They explained to Sacco that the structures were being used to access underground tunnels to smuggle weapons and ammunition into the region from nearby Egypt. In fact, the Israelis consider Rafah the most "active front." Still, Rafah is now home to more than 105,000 Palestinian refugees, surely not all of them terrorists. Some Palestinians, for instance, are forced from their homes due to constant Israeli gunfire. After they are gone, the American-made Caterpillar D9 bulldozers move in and pave over their homes, their belongings, and their lives, should they remain inside. Many Palestinians now feel that the Israelis are using the existence of the tunnels as an excuse to bulldoze more land, giving way to an extension of Israel's territory and settlements.

Yet another issue that concerns Palestinians is the current construction of a barrier wall in occupied Palestine. While Israel maintains that the wall is being built to help defend Israelis against further suicide attacks, the barrier, which could eventually extend over 466 miles (750 km), would separate the West Bank from Israel by consuming additional Palestinian land. If the Israelis complete the wall as planned, it will make it increasingly difficult for

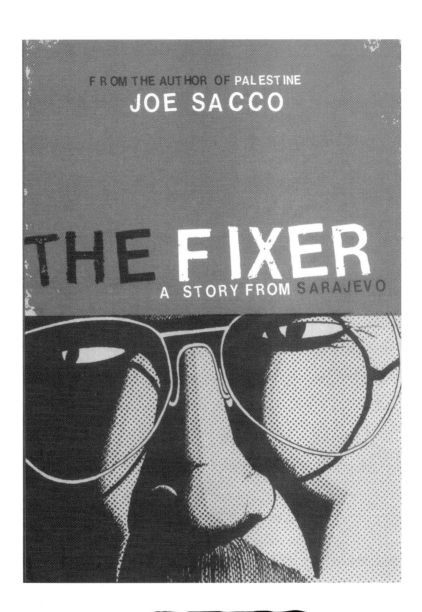

In this cover image of *The Fixer: A Story from Sarajevo*, Sacco offers an extreme close-up of his protagonist, Neven, a "fixer" whose job it is to offer information and services to foreign journalists in Bosnia who are searching for their news stories. In the story, Sacco meets Neven after the war is over and although he initially shakes Sacco down for cash, they eventually become friends and Neven tells him about his past and his involvement in the Bosnian war.

Palestinians to earn a living, go to school, or reach health care facilities.

Anger Generates Action

Although Sacco hoped to bring attention to the conflict by using comics in his journalism, he isn't totally certain that Americans are completely aware of these and other events like them around the world. In recent interviews, such as the one by Christopher Farah that appeared in www.salon.com at the end of 2003, Sacco was clearly outraged by what he perceives as American apathy.

"I think the American population should be sent to the Hague to be judged," he said. "This is a country that has an enormous impact around the world. What is decided in Washington D.C., when George Bush lifts his little finger—someone around the world is going to feel it. To me it seems almost criminal that the people who live here, who elect someone like that—if they really knew how other people's lives are affected by American policies, maybe they would pay more attention. It's appalling the amount of ignorance here about world events." In Sacco's opinion, anger generates action, something he hopes to inspire in the audience that reads his comic books.

Unending Conflict

At the time of this writing in 2004, the violence in Gaza has only intensified. Palestinian refugees are increasingly left without homes, proper medical care, food, water, or other necessary items, while civilian Israelis are often caught in the crossfire. And while Israelis are also victimized by the violent relationships between the two groups, Sacco sees the peace process as an unlikely one. He feels that the United States should be pressuring Israel to pull out of the area and return some of the land in order to help create an official Palestinian state. In 2004, he told the *Los Angeles Weekly*, "I was [in Gaza] several times over the past year, and during that year the level of violence went way up on both sides. It's no longer a question of police in Jeeps coming around and shooting a few rubber bullets—it's tanks and aircraft now. It looks increasingly likely that there won't be a viable Palestinian state, and that these two peoples will be forever conjoined in some way that might result in an Apartheid situation."

A recent incident of death and destruction in Gaza in mid-May 2004 at the hands of Israeli soldiers brought

Sacco covered the 2004 U.S. election in a series of comic strips that he drew for *Washington Monthly*, a politically liberal magazine, in 2004. In this excerpt, he wrote about how even ardent supporters of the Republican Party had their doubts about President George W. Bush's bid for reelection.

with it even more attention when thirty-four Palestinians were killed and hundreds of others were injured. The incident crippled Rafah's already weak hospital, which had an incredible time dealing with the onslaught of injured civilians.

Speaking to guests in New York City in 2004 at a panel discussion during the annual Museum of Comic and Cartoon Art Festival, Sacco graciously answered questions from the audience following a slide show of his illustrations. Sacco often uses such settings to explain his journalistic approach and offers insights into his process of writing and drawing that results in his unique form of accurate reporting, intimate storytelling, and exquisite illustration.

Within days, the United Nations took a vote and determined that the incident (Israeli troops allegedly opened fire on a group of 3,000 Palestinian protesters) was a human rights violation. While nearly all UN member countries decided that the strikes were unlawful, the United States abstained from voting at all.

It's violence like this that Sacco hopes will draw people's attention. In his current work, tentatively titled *One Day in Gaza*, possibly due out in 2006, he is again exploring places like Rafah. In other projects, Sacco is exploring the assault by the Russian army in Chechnya and the flight of Chechen refugees to Ingushetia. However, he does plan to eventually explore other, less intense subject matter. He is presently partnering with his friend Gerry Mohr from the Miracle Workers on a comic that profiles the history of the Rolling Stones (tentatively titled *the Gentleman's Guide to the Rolling Stones*), and one day, he claims he might try his hand at writing fiction. Sacco's current work can be found in the *Washington Monthly*, where he is a regular columnist/cartoonist writing about the 2004 U.S. presidential race. Another recent piece appeared in the quarterly publication *McSweeney's*, which, in issue 13, profiled North America's most accomplished comics artists.

Through the unique comics journalism genre that Sacco pioneered, his voice continues to draw much needed attention to global human rights issues. By reaching this growing audience, and continuing to chronicle the human condition in a compelling art form, Sacco is helping to unite people in a more thorough understanding of political strife around the world.

SELECTED WORKS

The Fixer: A Story from Sarajevo. Montreal, Canada: Drawn & Quarterly Publications, 2003.

Notes from a Defeatist. Seattle: Fantagraphics, 2003.

Palestine. Seattle: Fantagraphics Books, 2001.

Safe Area Gorazde: The War in Eastern Bosnia 1992–95. Seattle: Fantagraphics Books, 2000.

Soba: Stories From Bosnia. Montreal, Canada: Drawn & Quarterly Publications, 1998.

Spotlight on the Genius That Is Joe Sacco. Seattle: Fantagraphics Books, 1994.

War Junkie. Seattle: Fantagraphics Books, 1995.

Zero Zero, number 15. Seattle: Fantagraphics Books, 1997.

SELECTED AWARDS

American Book Award
Palestine, 1996

Eisner Award
Best Graphic Novel (*Safe Area Gorazde: The War in Eastern Bosnia 1992–1995* 2001)

Firecracker Award
Palestine, 2002

Guggenheim Fellowship (2001)

Harvey Award
Best Cartoonist (*Soba,* 1999)
Best One-Shot Comic (*Soba,* 1999)
Best Writer (*Soba,* 1999)

Ignatz Award
Outstanding Graphic Novel or Collection (*Safe Area Gorazde: The War in Eastern Bosnia 1992–1995,* 2001)

VPRO Grand Prix of Harlem Award
Palestine, 2002

GLOSSARY

Allied powers During World War II, the combined forces of Great Britain, France, the Soviet Union, and the United States.

apartheid A social policy of racial segregation involving political, economic, and legal discrimination.

Axis powers During World War II, the combined forces of Germany, Italy, and Japan.

Cold War A conflict of ideological differences carried on without full military action, and usually without breaking up diplomatic relationships. A condition of rivalry and distrust between the United States and the Soviet Union from the 1940s to the early 1990s.

Communism A political and economic system based on Marxism in which all property is shared.

diaspora The dispersion or spreading of a people who were originally localized in one area.

empathy Identification with and understanding of another's situation and feelings.

idyll A romantic scene or event of rustic simplicity.

incumbent A person who currently holds a position, usually used to describe a sitting president.

indigenous Native to an area, such as a person, his or her family, or a specific animal, plant, or tree.

insurgency Rising in revolt; rebellious.

intifada Palestinian uprising against Israeli oppression in the occupied territories.

martial law A system of rules that takes effect (usually after a formal declaration) when a particular situation requires that a military authority take control of the system of government (and usually the entire state).

napalm An aluminum soap that is mixed with gasoline to make a jelly. Napalm is often used in flamethrowers and fire bombs.

nationalism Loyalty and devotion to a nation, placing an emphasis on the promotion of its culture and interests above others.

pacifist A person who resists violence and war between people and nations.

raze To willfully tear down or demolish by force.

reprisal Retaliation for an injury with the intent of inflicting at least as much injury in return.

sequential Relating to the following of one thing after another; succession.

solidarity A unity of interests, purposes, or sympathies among a group of people.

sovereign Complete independence or self-government, usually used to describe a nation.

Amnesty International
322 Eighth Avenue
New York, NY 10001
(212) 807-8400
e-mail: admin-us@aiusa.org
Web site: http://amnestyusa.org

Comic Book Legal Defense Fund
P.O. Box 693
Northampton, MA 01061
(800) 992-2533
Web site: http://www.cbldf.org

The Comics Journal
7563 Lake City Way NE
Seattle, WA 98115
(800) 657-1100
(206) 524-1967
e-mail: fbicomix@fantagraphics.com
Web site: http://www.tcj.com/

Fantagraphics Books
7563 Lake City Way NE
Seattle, WA 98115
(800) 657-1100

(206) 524-1967
e-mail: fbicomix@fantagraphics.com
Web site: http://www.fantagraphics.com

Jewish Voice for Peace
1611 Telegraph Avenue, Suite 500
Oakland, CA 94612
(510) 465-1777
e-mail: info@jewishvoiceforpeace.org
Web site: http://www.jewishvoiceforpeace.org/

New York City Comic Book Museum
P.O. Box 230676
New York, NY 10023
(212) 712-9454
e-mail: nyccbm@hotmail.com
Web site: http://www.nyccomicbookmuseum.org/

In Canada

Drawn & Quarterly Publications
P.O. Box 48056
Montreal, Quebec, H2V 4S8
(514) 279-2221
Web site: http://www.drawnandquarterly.com/

Solidarity for Palestinian Human Rights
1118 St. Catherine West, Suite 405
Montreal, Quebec H3B 1H5
Web site: http://www.sphr.org/

Web Sites

Due to the changing nature of Internet links, the Rosen
Publishing Group, Inc., has developed an online list of
Web sites related to the subject of this book. This site is
updated regularly. Please use this link to access the list:

http://www.rosenlinks.com/lgn/josa

Murolo, Priscilla and A. B. Chitty (Illustrated by Joe Sacco). *From the Folks Who Brought You the Weekend: A Short Illustrated History of Labor in the United States*. New York: The New Press, 2001.

Sacco, Joe. *The Fixer: A Story from Sarajevo*. Montreal, Canada: Drawn & Quarterly Publications, 2003.

Sacco, Joe. *Notes from a Defeatist*. Seattle: Fantagraphics Books, 2003.

Sacco, Joe. *Palestine*. Seattle: Fantagraphics Books, 2003.

Sacco, Joe. *Safe Area Gorazde: The War in Eastern Bosnia 1992–95*. Seattle: Fantagaphics Books, 2003.

BIBLIOGRAPHY

Bennet, Kathleen E. "Joe Sacco's Palestine: Where Comics Meet Journalism," *The Stranger*. Retrieved January 2004 (http://www.drizzle.com/~kathleen/comix/sacco.html).

Binelli, Mark. "Joe Sacco's Cartoon Violence." *Rolling Stone*, January 22, 2004, pp. 40–41.

Blincoe, Nicholas. "Cartoon Wars: By Dramatizing Events in Comic Book Form, Joe Sacco Exposes the Fantasy of the Israeli Occupation (The Back Half)." *New Statesman*. Retrieved January 2004 (http://articles.findarticles.com/p/articles/mi_m0FQP/is_4619_132/ai_96736508).

Chiotti, Tony. "Drawing the Faceless," *Oregon Quarterly*. Retrieved February 2004 (http://darkwing.uoregon.edu/~oq/).

Giuffo, John. "Sacco in a Strange Land," *New York Review of Magazines*. Retrieved January 2004 (http://www.jrn.columbia.edu/studentwork/nyma-greview/features/sacco.html).

Groth, Gary. "Joe Sacco, Frontline Journalist: Why Sacco Went to Gorazde," *The Comics Journal*. Retrieved January 2004 (http://www.tcj.com/aa02ws/i_sacco.html).

Guardian Unlimited. "I Do Comics, Not Graphic Novels," Retrieved January 2004 (http://books.guardian.

co.uk/departments/politicsphilosophyandsociety/
story/0,6000,1069136,00.html).

Hedges, Chris (with illustrations by Joe Sacco). "A
Gaza Diary: Scenes from the Palestinian Uprising."
Harper's, October 2001, pp. 48–59.

Lalumière, Claude. "The Not-So-Comic Question of
Ethnic Nationalism," *January Magazine*. Retrieved
January 2004 (http://www.januarymagazine.com/
nonfiction/sacco.html).

McKenna, Kristine. "Brueghel in Bosnia," *Los Angeles
Weekly*. Retrieved January 2004 (http://www.laweekly.
com/ink/04/06/features-mckenna.php).

Morman, Todd. "Serious Comics," Independent Online.
Retrieved January 2004 (http://www.indyweek.com/
durham/2000-10-25/ae2.html).

Powers, Thom. "Joe Sacco Interview." *The Comics
Journal*, No. 176. April 1995.

Spurgeon, Tom. "Drawing the Line on War: Joe Sacco's
Comics Journalism Brings Bosnia to Life," *Portland
Mercury*, vol. 1, no. 3. Retrieved January 2004
(http://www.portlandmercury.com/
2000-06-15/books.html).

Thompson, David. "Eyewitness in Gaza," *The
Guardian*. Retrieved January 2004 (http://books.
guardian.co.uk/reviews/politicsphilosophyandsociety/
0,6121,868704,00.html).

Tuhus-Dubrow, Rebecca. "Joe Sacco," *January
Magazine*. Retrieved January 2004 (http://www.
januarymagazine.com/profiles/jsacco.html).

INDEX

About the Author

Monica Marshall is a freelance writer living in New York who has been known to enjoy a comic or two, especially those by Joe Sacco.

Acknowledgments

Many thanks to Gary Groth, Kim Thompson, and Eric Reynolds for their collective assistance in obtaining information about Joe Sacco and for their generosity in allowing us to reprint Sacco's drawings. For more information about Sacco, or other talented cartoonists featured in Fantagraphics Books, please visit the publisher's Web site www.fantagraphics.com. Finally, a special note of thanks to Joe Sacco himself, who provided both personal time and spirit to this project.

Credits

Cover (photo) © Sol Neelman, Cover (comics), pp, 5, 9, 11, 32, 34, 47, 50, 56, 58, 61, 75, 79, 80, 82, 85, 90, 97 © 2004 Joe Sacco; pp. 13, 19, 29 © Bettmann/Corbis; p. 22 Reproduced with permission, Macmillan UK; p. 41 © Jacob Covey; p. 44 courtesy Fantagraphics Books, Seattle, WA; p. 67 © Francoise de Mulder/Corbis; p. 68 © Peter Turnley/Corbis; p. 77 Courtesy of Joe Sacco; p. 93 Copyright © 2001 *From the Folks Who Brought You the Weekend: A Short, Illustrated History of Labor in the United States* by Priscilla Murolo, A.B. Chitty, illustrations by Joe Sacco. Reprinted by permission of The New Press. 800-233-4830; p. 95 Used with permission, Drawn & Quarterly, Montréal, Québec; p. 98 © Joann Jovinelly

Designer: Les Kanturek; Editor: Joann Jovinelly